The Restoration and Conservation of Islamic Monuments in Egypt

Edited by
Jere L. Bacharach

The American University in Cairo Press

The American Research Center in Egypt gratefully acknowledges the following
financial contributions:

*To the International Conference on the Restoration and Conservation of Islamic
Monuments in Egypt, 12–15 June 1993, Cairo:*
United States Information Agency
Egyptian Antiquities Organization
Getty Conservation Institute
European Research Office, United States Army

To the publication of this work:
Samuel H. Kress Foundation
Middle East Center, Jackson School of International Studies, University of
Washington

The American Research Center in Egypt also wishes to acknowledge the
contributions of Professor Jere L. Bacharach to the success of the conference and
the subsequent publication of its proceedings.

Dar el Kutub No. 8748/94
ISBN 977 424 356 0

Library of Congress Cataloging-in-Publication Data:

94-961128

The restoration and conservation of Islamic monuments in Egypt / edited by Jere L.
Bacharach. — [Cairo] : American University in Cairo Press, 1995.
p. ;   cm.

Printed in Egypt at the Printshop of the American University in Cairo

Contents

Preface

Where were you during the *zilzal?* For many residents of Cairo, the earthquake of 12 October 1992 marked a fundamental change in their lives. In addition to the human tragedies, worldwide attention was drawn to the Islamic monuments of Egypt, particularly in Cairo, where the collapse of one dome and the precariousness of many minarets made the preservation of the Islamic heritage an international issue. In addition to the immediate response of local organizations and institutions such as the Egyptian Antiquities Organization (EAO) and the German Archaeological Institute (DAI), international missions quickly arrived. The American Research Center in Egypt (ARCE) suddenly found itself playing an active role welcoming these missions and putting them in touch with appropriate local authorities.

Among the groups aided by ARCE was a team of specialists on seismic retrofit from the University of Michigan, a group of earthquake-damage specialists from the National Park Service, and an international team associated with the U.S. Army Corps of Engineers. A team of British scholars working for UNESCO on the Giza plateau also surveyed the damage to the Islamic and Coptic monuments of Cairo.

At the same time, Mark Easton, Cairo Director of ARCE, and I began discussing the possibility of holding an ARCE-sponsored conference devoted to the conservation and preservation of Islamic monuments in Egypt. The original funding for the gathering came from a United States Information Agency grant awarded to ARCE for the purpose of holding a conference in Cairo. Through the efforts of Easton, Terry Walz, Executive Director of ARCE, and myself, additional funding was acquired from the European Research Office, the U.S. Army, the Getty Conservation Institute, and ARCE's own coffers. Sponsors of the conference included ARCE, the EAO, and the Getty Conservation Institute. In March 1993 Barbara Fudge of Cairo joined me as conference coordinator. Later, engineer Ibrahim Sadek, in his capacity as acting director of ARCE-Cairo, played an important role in furthering the goals of the conference.

The ARCE team sought to make the conference as inclusive as possible, both in terms of disciplines and nationalities. In seeking Egyptian specialists, Hassanein Rabie, then Dean of the College of Arts at Cairo University, played a critical role. Not only were faculty from his college included, but members of the College of Archaeology, and the relatively new Engineering Center for Archaeology and Environment, College of Engineering, Cairo University were on the program. Mahmoud Nabil of the Engineering Center deserves a special word of thanks for his help in the conference and the book. Other Egyptians representing the EAO, Assiut University, and private enterprise joined the proceedings as presenters of papers. In 1978 a conference on a similar theme was held in which one out of the fourteen papers was given by an Egyptian; in the 1993 ARCE conference sixteen of twenty-nine presenters were Egyptian nationals. In the 1993 conference approximately half of the papers were given by engineers and scientists, while at the 1978 meeting only art historians, historians, and restorers presented papers.

The conference was held from 12 to 15 June at the American University in Cairo's Jameel Center. An esprit de corps was established immediately among the participants, which was carried throughout the conference. The goals and spirit of the conference were captured in the introductory remarks by Mark Easton and Jane Slate Siena, of the Getty Conservation Institute, which have been included in this volume. In fact, one major success of the gathering was the degree to which specialists were able and willing to exchange information and ideas with their counterparts from around the world. The audience, ranging from sixty to over one hundred members, also joined in the formal and informal discussions.

The presentations highlighted many of the issues that have been discussed at length by those concerned with the fate of Cairo's Islamic monuments. Problems of the water table, sewage, urban traffic, and so on— all of which can be found in the UNESCO report of 1980 and in the SPARE newsletters—were emphasized, as well as newer problems resulting from the earthquake, the creation of the underground tunnel for the Metro, and lowering the water table around a historic site too quickly.

The last morning of the conference was set aside for workshops: (1) Urban Management, Training Programs, and Institutional Strengthening; (2) Buildings as Archaeology and Sustainable Use; (3) Identification of Historical Buildings and Documentation as a Public Resource; (4) Technologies for Repair. These were followed by a plenary session in which each group presented a series of resolutions, which were then voted upon by all those in attendance. The resolutions of the 1993 International Conference on the Restoration and Conservation of Islamic Monuments in Egypt can be found at the end of this book.

In the year and three months since the conference there have been a number of developments which are worth noting as positive signs for the future. The U.S. government, through its Agency for International Development (USAID) awarded ARCE a large grant for the restoration and conservation of Egypt's heritage. Work has already begun on one Islamic monument. In September 1994 a UNDP-sponsored sustainable development program in Egypt conference was held under the directorship of Dr. Adli Bishay. Extensive material for preservation and conservation of Islamic monuments in the Gamaliyya district of Cairo and in Rosetta (Rashid) was presented.

Facing a pressing deadline and financial constraints, I was rather suddenly asked to edit the papers that had been submitted by contributors to the conference. I turned to Felicia J. Hecker, director of the Near and Middle East Publications Program at the University of Washington, for help. With incredible energy and skill, she transformed the numerous conference papers into this book. Fortunately we were aided by Mark Easton and Barbara Fudge in Cairo who responded rapidly to our requests. In addition, important contributions were made by Jim Sorenson and Ibrahim Sadek.

Funding for this volume was made possible through grants from the United States Information Agency and the Middle East Center, the Jackson School of International Studies, the University of Washingon. Deadlines forced certain editorial decisions for which I take full responsibility. We were not able to send proofs to the authors, so I apologize for any errors in their papers since they did not have the opportunity to check them.

The papers submitted have been grouped under two different headings, "Restoration" and "Conservation." These divisions are porous as many of the articles on restoration include important information on conservation, and vice versa. The papers reflect the diversity of disciplines involved in and concerned with the heritage of Islamic Egypt and include archaeologists, art historians, architects, administrators, and a wide range of engineers. It is appropriate that almost half the authors are Egyptians, and that they have been joined by individuals from Britain, Germany, Italy, Poland, Turkey, and the United States. The book concludes with the conference resolutions and a list of the contributors.

—Jere L. Bacharach

Urban Memory and the Preservation of Monuments

Irene A. Bierman

The monuments of a memory map create a realized past essential to a vital present and future. But not all buildings are monuments, and no map is the territory. Monuments keep the dead from wholly dying. Through them we preserve what we wish to remember. Monuments are also instruments of forgetting. They keep the other beyond the threshold of memory. Creswell's twentieth-century maps of Muhammadan monuments of Cairo, David Roberts' nineteenth-century drawings of Cairo's buildings and neighborhoods, and al-Maqrizi's descriptions of the fifteenth-century *khitat* of Cairo are some of the most famous traditional maps of the area, and they do serve to keep the city in our memory. Territory, however, is more than a map. It is a lived experience. My focus here is how the lived experience of Cairo has been punctuated by those agents of memory we call monuments.[1] What is preserved in the territory creates the sensory map for those who traverse the ground.

The memory map of Cairo has been created by historical layering, a continuous process affected by natural and social forces. A natural force like an earthquake disrupts the days and ways, leaving in its wake deaths, broken lives, broken hopes, shaken buildings and monuments. In 1304 a great quake shook the streets of Cairo, killing many and tumbling the tops off the minarets on the Shari' al-'Azam, the Great Street, running from the Bab al-Futuh to the Bab Zuwayla and beyond. According to the written sources, no minaret on that street survived undamaged by the quake. The damage caused by the earthquake prompted a response from the Mamluk rulers that altered, among many things, the aesthetic quality of this central north–south axis of medieval Cairo. Rather than restoring them to their pre-earthquake form, repairs and restorations made to the minarets were accomplished in Mamluk style. Today, the effects of those decisions are most apparent on the mosque of al-Hakim, where Mamluk tops still surmount Fatimid bases.

In their own way social forces make change more powerfully, if more slowly. They leave their marks in different ways. On the one hand, buildings disappear from the urban fabric as a result of complex shifts in the socioeconomic underpinnings of society. Buildings lose their functional importance within a region. *Kharaba*, a medieval term signifying ruins, reflects the concern of the medieval writers about the disruption caused to urban life by the presence of so many buildings, formerly functional, falling into decay.[2] *Kharaba*, widely used in the pages of the Geniza documents of the twelfth century, and in later centuries by al-Maqrizi and Ibn Duqmaq, is a sign for the widespread complaints about the ruins, then often filled with garbage, that adjoined, faced, or were in the vicinity of inhabited structures in the urban area of medieval Cairo. Such shifts in the lived experience of the urban area result from many individual decisions rather than deliberate planning.

Deliberate planning to shape the city of Cairo, with attention to its aesthetic form, has traditionally been the act of the ruling power. As with all cities until recent times, government was the most active social force in managing urban form. From its founding by the Fatimids (or before that the Tulunids, or even before by the early Muslim forces under 'Amr ibn al-'As, if we consider the medieval twin cities as a whole) what was built and where, its aesthetic quality, and who could walk where and when, were decisions of those who ruled. Likewise, acting to preserve buildings and incorporating them into the legible infrastructure of the city was also the prerogative of rule. Each group in turn that ruled in Cairo rewrote history expressed in space by selectively shaping and transforming the visual urban memory, creating new conditions of legibility for the map.

"What time is this place?" Kevin Lynch asked when discussing questions of restoration and preservation of urban space.[3] The form of that question may belong to the end of the twentieth century, but ruling groups have always acted out the answer that the city and its memory map belong to its present inhabitants. Consider how the memory map of Cairo was shaped by the Ayyubid (A.D. 1171–1250/A.H. 564–650) and Mamluk (A.D. 1250–1517/A.H. 648–922) rulers. They inherited a walled region known as al-Qahira in which four sites formed a topography of rule and ceremonial that served the hegemonic purposes of the Fatimid Isma'ili caliphs and the ruling group that supported them. All four sites were located in the northern half of the city: the Bayn al-Qasrayn and the two palaces creating it; the mosque of al-Hakim at Bab al-Futuh; the *musalla* at Bab al-Nasr; and the mosque of al-Azhar.

The central locus of Fatimid rule and ideology was formed by the two palaces and the area between them known by this relationship, Bayn al-Qasrayn (between the two palaces). The ruling caliph resided in the eastern and larger palace complex. There too the previous Isma'ili imams were interred. Other members of the ruling family, often the heir apparent, resided across Bayn al-Qasrayn in the smaller palace on the western side. The central networks of relationships came together in this site. Required by their belief to see the ruling imam during their lifetime, Isma'ili Muslims could view the imam in Bayn al-Qasrayn where the ruler and his entourage presented themselves to the public on ceremonial occasions. There, too, all members of the society, not simply the Isma'ili Muslims, could view the Fatimid caliph and present him with petitions. There people put on plays and dances. Even when the caliph did not come into the space, those assembled viewed him in the window above the *bab al-dhahab*, the main palace gate that opened onto the Bayn al-Qasrayn. Processions and ceremonials began in the Bayn al-Qasrayn, and important visitors came through this space to the *bab al-dhahab*.[4] The three other sites that made up the topography of rule were located to the north and south of this area.

A short distance to the south, east off the main north–south street, was the major Isma'ili jami': the mosque of al-Azhar, the site of lectures on Isma'ili beliefs, and the space for Friday prayers for the residents of the walled city. The eastern palace was connected by an underground tunnel to this mosque so that there was direct and hidden access to and from the palace. North of the palace area were located two other gathering spaces for prayer important in the Fatimid ceremonial use of the city: the mosque of al-Hakim at Bab al-Futuh, and the *musalla* at Bab al-Nasr. At the mosque of al-Hakim, the court assembled for prayer before the start of Friday processions. There the caliph was unveiled as he sat in the minbar to deliver the *khutba*. The *musalla*, not a building but rather a delineated space, was used for prayers during important celebrations of the Isma'ili calendar, such as the birthdays of the imams.

The Ayyubid and then the early Mamluk rulers maintained three of these sites as part of their own topography of rule, and thus fixed these locations on their memory map of Cairo. However, they effectively inscribe these locations within different aesthetic, social and structural networks, layering these sites with historical associations of rule.[5] Al-Azhar mosque became the foremost jami' of the Mamluk empire. Ayyubid and then Mamluk rulers transformed it into the center par excellence of Sunni spiritual life. This social transformation was paralleled by a formal transformation. Minarets, halls, entrances, and mausolea transformed the internal spaces as well as the façade of this mosque. In aesthetic terms, al-Azhar lost its resemblance to its Fatimid form. The name al-Azhar, once a sign of Isma'ili Shi'i prayer and learning, became a name associated, as it is today, with Sunni learning.

The prayer spaces in the north were also transformed. One, the *musalla*, has been lost to public memory. Mamluk period historians such as al-Maqrizi and Ibn Duqmaq make it known to us today. But by the Mamluk period that space had become part of the open area, *rahba*, a parade ground for the Mamluk troops who often paraded into the walled city through the Bab al-Nasr. The building of the mosque of al-Hakim, its external form as well as the internal spatial relationships, was preserved, and even restored after the 1304 earthquake, although as mentioned above the minaret tops were reshaped. While the structure was maintained, the social role was changed, as was its position within the hierarchy of important sites in the city. In

Mamluk times it was endowed with professorships in each of the four Sunni schools, and while important in the academic life of the city, it played a role of lesser importance than al-Azhar and those institutions at Bayn al-Qasrayn.[6]

Bayn al-Qasrayn and the two palaces were transformed socially, structurally, and aesthetically, yet the location remained important in the new hierarchy of centers within the city. The palaces may have continued to be inhabited in the early Ayyubid period, but first on the west side of Bayn al-Qasrayn, and then on the east the palaces were soon demolished, a process that changed the shape of Bayn al-Qasrayn itself. The madrasa of al-Kamil Ayyub (A.D. 1229/A.H. 626) was built in part of the area of the western palace, an overlay that was completed in the Mamluk period with the construction of the complexes and mausolea of Sultan Qalawun, and Sultan al-Nasir Muhammad. On the east side, the Fatimid imam's residence and the mausoleum of the Ismai'li imams was replaced by the madrasa and mausoleum complex of Najm al-Din Ayyub. This whole area remained residential in character as it had been, but in Ayyubid and Mamluk times the residents were the students and professors at the great academic institutions that shaped the space. The area also remained the burial site of the rulers, as Ayyubid and then Mamluk rulers were buried there. The graves of the Fatimid imams, however, were torn up and the remains scattered. Although the shape of Bayn al-Qasrayn was ultimately altered by these new constructions, the name persists until today, carrying with it the memory of the palaces and, perhaps more than that, the public activities that took place in the space.[7]

The memory map of Cairo was shaped by more than the acts of former rulers. These last years of the twentieth century bring an acute awareness of the multiplicity of social forces shaping urban geography.[8] Worldwide disciplinary knowledge, senses of professionalism in urban planning and design and other professions have structured and restructured urban space. Further, our attention has been drawn recently to the role of architectural drawings, of surveys and compendia, of postcard views, and of World's Fairs in shaping memory maps.[9] I turn now to one example of how our memory map of Cairo was constituted by decisions made within the last one hundred years or so.[10] The very processes of forgetting and remembering that shaped the territory of the site of rule we have been discussing was framed largely by actions taken by the Comité de conservation des monuments de l'art arabe (Comité).[11]

In the early 1880s the Comité, composed of Egyptians and foreign nationals (mainly French and British), drew up a list of what it termed noteworthy buildings of Arab art. More than six hundred buildings were on that list, most of which were located in the urban area from Ahmad ibn Tulun in the south to Bab al-Futuh in the north, roughly an area of four square kilometers. In the 1890s, old Coptic churches and monasteries—most of which were in Fustat, or Misr al-Qadima, were added to this list, thus extending the area under consideration roughly another kilometer southward. For working purposes, the Comité divided this large list of monuments into two categories: those from the Fatimid period (A.D. 969–1171/A.H. 359–567) and earlier, relatively few in number, were to be worked on first and preserved, and those more numerous monuments from the Mamluk and Ottoman periods, because of their large number, could be treated with more latitude. André Raymond's recent work has indicated that roughly an equal number of Mamluk and Ottoman monuments remained, but more Mamluk buildings were put on the monuments list than Ottoman ones. A brief word or two more, however, needs to be said about the monument list, and the bases of this division, so that now, more than a century later, we can understand the modern memory map of Cairo.

From the Comité's point of view, important buildings of the eighteenth and nineteenth centuries were too new for inclusion in the list, and of course, our century, the twentieth century, was yet to arrive, and the major Art Deco period buildings in Cairo had yet to be built. The dichotomy the Comité created between Fatimid and earlier buildings on the one hand, and Mamluk and Ottoman ones on the other, led to some decisions in restoration that we need to acknowledge. One network of interrelated examples will help explore some of those decisions. The Comité set about almost immediately to conserve and restore to their "original" form the Fatimid buildings on the Great Street, Shari' al-'Azam, its medieval name, that is, the street running from Bab al-Futuh to Bab Zuwayla and beyond. At that time five Fatimid period buildings remained on the east side of the street: the mosque of al-Hakim, the mosque of al-Aqmar, the mosque of al-Azhar, the mosque of al-Fakahani , and the mosque of Salih Tala'i'.

Many decisions were made to accomplish effectively their express purpose of returning these buildings to their Fatimid state—and I will mention just a few recorded in the minutes of the Comité's meetings. The exterior of the mosque of al-Hakim was left virtually intact in its present state, that is, the present state of the turn of the century, with the minaret tops from the Mamluk restorations after the 1304 earthquake, and the Mamluk mausoleum in front of the main door.[12] On the other hand, the existing minaret on the mosque of Salih Tala'i', a typical Ottoman conical form seen elsewhere in the city, which had been put up after the eighteenth-century earthquake by the Ottoman governor, was taken down. The plan was to restore the minaret on the mosque with a "pure" Fatimid minaret form. Since, of course, no one knew what the original minarets looked like, and all remaining Fatimid minarets in Egypt differ in form from one another, the discussions about how to proceed were heated. Significantly, the minutes of these meetings of the Comité indicate that some members of the group wanted to establish symbolic forms for each historic period, and wanted the group to establish on this street the exemplar Fatimid form. Years of discussion went by as a consensus of what constituted a pure Fatimid form eluded the Comité.[13] Some wanted to replicate the minaret of al-Guyushi's complex; others the

Fatimid minaret in Luxor, and still others wanted to fabricate a combination composed of parts of both. Other members of the Comité were unwilling to adopt such a method of conservation. The discussions about what actions to take, deadlocked as they were, went on so long that World War II intervened, and no minaret was put on the building. Consequently, today's pedestrian on this street sees the composite minaret of the mosque of al-Hakim (Fatimid base, Mamluk top), and no minaret on that of Salih Tala'i'. Few then realize that this mosque had a minaret over its doorway from the time of its construction in the twelfth century A.D./fifth century A.H., until its restoration by the Comité at the beginning of this century. These methods of establishing a pure form for a given period were also applied to Mamluk restoration. Without belaboring these beginnings any further, let us understand them as a reminder that preservation of points on the memory map is always a complex issue, now as well as then, as well as in the Mamluk and Ottoman periods, as in the postmodern.

We can examine some of these issues in more abstract terms. Historical layering in the visible city is a continuous process. Formal architectural elements relate to each other in two kinds of distinct, yet overlapping, semi-autonomous ways. One process involves the relationship between the exterior façade and the interior space of a building. Historical layering also involves the semi-autonomy of forms. Publicly visible architectural elements are appropriated and assigned new meanings or connotation. The two elements, exterior façade and interior space, relate to social processes at different rates, and not in tandem. Interior elements of buildings are always most elusive, and usually subject to more continual transformations and adaptive reuse. Take, for example, the mosque of al-Hakim. While the exterior remained relatively stable, delimiting the passage from the city at Bab al-Futuh, the interior which began as a mosque built by the Fatimid dynasty in the late tenth century, has served variously since then as a madrasa, a girl's school, and by Comité direction, the first location of the Museum of Arab Art; it is now once again functioning as a mosque. When the interiors of buildings are not adapted in reuse—and not all will have such dramatic shifts as the interior of al-Hakim's mosque—then buildings become ruins. Ruins in a city are the public signal of significant social and cultural change in the expectations of interior spaces and the patterning of use of such spaces. The semi-autonomy of a building (its exterior façade and its interior space) enables each to have separate trajectories. After all, interiors of buildings rarely become national emblems, but exteriors do.

Exteriors of buildings give definition to street patterns and are often maintained for that reason long after the interiors have lost their active social function. In neighborhoods where monuments cluster, the way the façades of structures of differing periods abut the space of the street enables the pedestrian, and today also the driver, to sense the different historical practices relating to street space through the varying proportions of the street. Nowhere is this clearer than in Bayn al-Qasrayn. Today we see and feel the Mamluk and Ayyubid three-dimensionality of this street as we walk from the gold-sellers area and jog slightly left to proceed up north to Bab al-Futuh. The historical richness of Cairo is impressed on people who walk these streets whether or not they know the period or style of the buildings. The alternative to this rich three-dimensional layering is those sections of Cairo, and of other contemporary cities, where zoning and set back requirements impose a uniformity on the street grid.

With much evidence to back us from the writings of Ibn Duqmaq and al-Maqrizi on, we could argue that streets rather than buildings are the main feature of the memory map of Cairo.[14] Members of the Egyptian government in the late 1880s chose to represent old Cairo in just such a fashion at the World's Columbian Exhibition in 1893.[15] The only recognizable building that was replicated on this street was the sabil–kuttab of 'Abd al-Rahman Katkhuda (A.D. 1744/A.H. 1157). Not the building to serve as an emblem of Cairo that architectural historians might choose, it nevertheless is the building that conspicuously serves to narrow and to shape Shari' al-'Azam as one travels north along the road (fig. 1). A full-scale replica of the sabil–kuttab was built on the Street of Old Cairo in the Fair (fig. 2) and it functioned there as the original did—it narrowed the street and served as a focal point. One function of the building was misunderstood by many readers and journalists; it was described as an "ancient mosque," and a "house with balconies."[16] Its aesthetic form stood as a symbol of narrow streets, and of activities appropriate to such streets. Five times a day a wedding procession complete with camels and howdah, donkeys, bells, drums, and colorful textiles wound its way through the replicated street of old Cairo. The Street of Old Cairo, so different in proportion to the late nineteenth-century streets of urban American cities, and its hubbub of activities was one of the most popular sections of the World's Fair, which drew 27.5 million visitors between May and October 1893. It was the Cairo they remembered.

One exterior feature, minarets, even when their interior stairs are no longer used, serves an important neighborhood function. Minarets can be seen not just from the elevated citadel, or from isolated viewpoints within the city, they can also be seen from within the neighborhood streets. The top of the tower helps to direct the pedestrian. Indeed, the distinctive tops that come from different periods serve to distinguish as well as connect areas, and serve to orient the viewer within a neighborhood, because most neighborhoods in this area have more than one minaret. In this sense, their presence, as well as their distinctive styles, are emblems of neighborhoods. In fact, we could with some historical justification claim that others outside Egypt understood how towers could serve an orientation function within a city. Pope Sixtus V, in the sixteenth century, placed a dozen Egyptian obelisks around the city of Rome so that, like minarets, they could guide pilgrims from afar, as well as near, to neighborhoods where the churches had the stations of the cross. Pilgrims without guidebooks simply needed to follow the obelisk tops, much as pedestrians had long been doing in many cities in Muslim territories. In the electronic age, this important function of a minaret as a guide or visual marker may be tempting to overlook. Indeed, into the premodern period, what this tower indicated was a prayer space, and a center for Muslim communal activities of various kinds. Many such buildings, with interiors that have remained unused, are now filling up again as Muslim communal activities are increasing, renewing the minaret as an important and complex neighborhood index.

We now turn to the second semi-autonomous way in which historical layering is made visible in the city—that process in which newly created old forms are used to fabricate a Cairene past and make linkages to it. In the building practices of the people of the city of Cairo, respect for older, publicly visible architectural elements has long been demonstrated by the appropriation of old forms to which new meanings or connotations have been assigned. The specific function of the old form is replaced by its function as a symbol referring to the already existing form, and thus symbolizing Cairene antiquity. Nowhere is this process clearer than in the appropriation of the form of the façade of the twelfth-century Fatimid al-Aqmar mosque by the Coptic community in making the new version the façade of the Coptic Museum in Misr al-Qadima (figs. 3 and 4). On the one hand, having two similar façades in the city enables us to see one as old and one as new, even though they are both present in our contemporary life.[17] Separated by almost five kilometers, the two structures are not frequented by the same Cairenes. Clearly the meanings evoked by the original façade in its twelfth-century context are not operative with regard to the façade of the museum. That this façade was an appropriate and acceptable choice as an echo of Cairene antiquity serves to highlight for us how architectural forms can become modern emblems of the historical past of Cairo. The sense of touch to the historical past is maintained and made relevant to its new uses, in this structure by the addition of writing in Coptic (language and alphabet) on the outside, along with the placement and use of Arabic as on the mosque of al-Aqmar.

The most consistent and visually prominent source for the appropriation of old forms has been the mosque of Sultan Hasan finished in A.D. 1363/764 A.H. 1363. In part because of its site at the foot of the citadel, on the road to the Qarafa, in part because of the scale of the building, and in part because of the excellence of the design and workmanship of this building, from the sixteenth century on it has served as a building to be emulated. In A.D. 1568, Mahmud Pasha, the Ottoman governor, built his mosque mausoleum with the same silhouette as that of Sultan Hasan. Anyone leaving the citadel, where the Ottoman palace and administration buildings were located, could not fail to notice the resonance of form. In fact, at some places on the road, the difference in scale between the two buildings allows the later building exactly to superimpose itself visually over the earlier one. Of course, the Ottoman-style minaret reminds the viewer of a different hand at work.

From the early years of this century, the mosque of al-Rifaʻi, completed in 1915, stands as the prominent example of the appropriation of structural forms from Sultan Hasan's complex across the street, as well as from other structures in the Mamluk period in general. Even the ornamental detailing of this mosque was consciously taken from a variety of mosques already existing in the city. Thus, in the early twentieth century—almost four hundred years after the end of the Mamluk period—a neo-Mamluk design was chosen as a mosque-mausoleum complex where King Fuad, as well as Shaykh ʻAli Rifaʻi, head of the Rifaʻi takiya, were buried. The mausolea of Sayyida Zaynab and Sayyida Nafisa were subsequently constructed in a similar neo-Mamluk style. Now, at the end of the twentieth century, what appears to be a post neo-Mamluk style for mosque-building is appearing in newer areas of Cairo. This style consciously refers to two historical layerings— one to the neo-Mamluk buildings of earlier this century, and the other to buildings of the Mamluk historical period. All three are contemporary in Cairo, but the appropriation of form is carried a step further in these more recent mosque buildings. From the exterior, the dome resonates recognizably in silhouette and surface design with Mamluk dome-forms across the wide expanse of this city. But the Mamluk domes to which these new ones refer covered mausoleum spaces, not spaces of communal prayer. Thus, one function of the Mamluk dome has been altered—indicating the presence of a mausoleum—while others continue. New meanings and new uses are assigned to old forms creating a twentieth-century connotative or symbolic system that is Cairene.

Big cities and old cities—and Cairo is both of these—are rich and complex, and because of this are especially in need of agents of memory, monuments, and memory mappings. They need to have a connecting thread, a perspective, a discourse, as Italo Calvino described it.[18] In other words: the visible city, the constructed universe, is a principle factor in engendering this connecting thread, this perspective and discourse. It provides the urban dweller a sense of community and continuity, a consciousness of the present, socially supported, engendered and reinforced by the visible city. Agents of memory, monuments, are vital for enhancing the complexity and significance of the present—our own sense of modernity. They make visible the process of change in the built environment, the visible city. We put them on our memory map because they have a present value as well as a maintenance of a sense of continuity.

Notes

1. For memory and mapping of cities see, Italo Calvino, *Invisible Cities* (Harcourt Brace Jovanovich, 1974); and Anthony Vidler, *The Architectural Uncanny*, (Cambridge: MIT Press, 1992), pp. 177–86.
2. S. D. Goitein, *A Mediterranean Society*, (Berkeley: University of California Press, 1983). Vol. 4 has a section on the city and on ruins within it (pp. 1–47).

3. Kevin Lynch, *What Time is This Place?* (Cambridge: MIT Press, 1972).

4. Ibn Duqmaq and al-Maqrizi are the Mamluk period sources for Fatimid ceremonial. See also Paula Sanders, *Ritual, Politics and the City in Fatimid Cairo* (Albany: State University of New York Press, 1994).

5. For an exploration of aspects of this issue in relation to Istanbul see Speros Vryonis,"Byzantine Constantinople and Ottoman Istanbul: Evolution in a Millenial Imperial Iconography," in *The Ottoman City and Its Parts*, edited by Irene A. Bierman, Rifa'at A. Abou-El-Haj and Donald Preziosi (New Rochelle: Aristide D. Caratzas, 1991), pp. 13–52.

6. For a guide to the hierarchy of institutions see Carl F. Petry, *The Civilian Elite of Cairo in the Later Middle Ages* (Princeton: Princeton University Press, 1981), appendix I.

7. Recent excavations directed by Nairy Hampikian of the German Archaeological Institute have uncovered walls of the eastern Fatimid palace. The trajectory of these walls suggest that Bayn al-Qasrayn had a different configuration from the present one.

8. Edward W. Soja, *Postmodern Geographies* (London: Verso, 1989) offers a summary of critical positions relating to space and a deeper look into social issues and the city of Los Angeles, which is illuminating.

9. See Anthony Vidler, *The Architectural Uncanny,* especially pp. 177–87 where he discusses monuments in western urban practice.

10. See especially Homi K. Bhabha, "DissemiNation: Time, Narrative, and the Margins of the Modern Nation," in *Nation and Narration,* edited by Homi K. Bhabha (London: Routledge, 1990), pp. 291–322.

11. Donald Malcolm Reid, "Cultural Imperialism and Nationalism: The Struggle to Define and Control the Heritage of Arab Art in Egypt," *International Journal of Middle East Studies* 24 (1992): 57–76. This article offers insights into the workings of this committee from its creation until the 1950s.

12. This mausoleum was moved to the northern cemetery in the 1980s.

13. See the minutes of the Comité: *Comité de conservation des monuments de l'art arabe* 28 (1911): 22; 29 (1912): 81; 32A (1915–19): 550–51; 36 (1930–32): 96–98; 103–19; 108–19; 38 (1936–40): 275–76; 39 (1941–45): 56.

14. For both Ibn Duqmaq and al-Maqrizi the urban armature is streets (of varying sizes). Their texts take us street by street (and then building by building) through the twin cities of Misr and Cairo.

15. Streets were also presented in the Paris exhibition. See Timothy Mitchell, "The World as Exhibition," *Comparative Studies in Society and History* 31.2 (1989):217–36.

16. See especially, Marian Shaw, *World's Fair Notes: A Woman Journalist's Views of Chicago's 1893 Columbian Exposition* (Pogo Press, 1992), pp. 56–60.

17. In this sense, of course, we could argue that they are both contemporary buildings.

18. Italo Calvino, *Invisible Cities.*

Fig. 2. Replica of the sabil–kuttab of 'Abd al-Rahman Katkhuda for the 1893 World Columbian Exhibition.

Fig. 1. The sabil–kuttab of 'Abd al-Rahman Katkhuda.

Fig. 3. Façade of the mosque of al-Aqmar.

Fig. 4. Façade of the Coptic Museum, Cairo.

Conservation Priorities in Cairo Today

Daryl Fowler

Cairo is a World Heritage city, enshrined on the list among seventy other cities that form UNESCO's World Heritage list. It contains possibly the finest collection of monuments in the Islamic world. Any work on the monuments must therefore measure up against the international standards that have been set by the various charters. Perhaps the most significant of these charters, for Cairo, are the Washington Historic Towns Charters and the *Charter of Venice*, which set out the basic principles for repairing and conserving historic monuments. The problems that face historic Cairo, however, extend far beyond the monuments.

What are to be the priorities for the problems that face Cairo? First of all we have the cultural imperative. Cairo contains some of the best surviving monuments of the medieval period in the Islamic world. The wealth, prosperity, and power of Cairo are reflected in the grand architecture of the monuments that are crowded together into the Fatimid city and just beyond. Second is the political imperative. The earthquake and its immediate consequences have meant that, possibly for the first time in several generations, we have obtained a strategic view of the condition of these monuments.

This then brings us to the third imperative, their physical condition. Buildings do not stand forever if they are not looked after, generations of neglect have resulted in almost every building being in urgent need of repair. Now, following the earthquake, there are very real problems. Fortunately, not many of the buildings collapsed during the recent earthquake, but many are now extremely vulnerable and fragile and clearly will not withstand the next earthquake.

What then of the institutional capacity? Cairo is a complicated city by anybody's standards. The Egyptian Antiquities Organization (EAO) has the primary role in caring for the monuments but, it seems, so has the user, the waqf holder in some cases. In addition, the various urban planning structures that exist within Cairo all have a significant role to play in the decision-making process.

There is no question that the EAO has the pedigree and the skilled practitioners within its ranks to carry out a formidable task; a task that, frankly, I do not relish. However, the very linear structure of management within the EAO is perhaps an impediment to success. The high political profile that the chairman has adopted has meant that any action, or lack of action, is likely to be in the headlines. There are times when the best conservation activity is no action at all. At the moment this is not one of those times.

The planners have their own problems. The conservation of historic Cairo has been an item on the international agenda for some twenty-five years but, as yet, we have actually achieved very little. Minor works have been carried out, individual monuments have been repaired by international agencies, but there has been little in the way of coordinated activities. The setting up of the organization for the renewal of the Fatimid city is a step in the right direction. But the term "renewal" is perhaps the wrong choice. We don't need to renew the Fatimid city, we just have to look after what is there and make the most of a world-class resource.

In the current framework, the construction industry too has problems. There is a lack of recent precedent in the repair of standing, traditional structures in Cairo. The business of repairing standing stone buildings is well-established in many countries throughout the world. Many of the techniques involved are no longer part of the modern construction industry's vocabulary. Despite the advertising placards around Cairo that proclaim "concrete" as the masculine look, "improving" these buildings with steel and with Portland cement is not good conservation practice. You have only to look at the Blue Mosque to see the problems of the future. So, as a part of these activities to repair and conserve historic Cairo, there are enormous challenges and opportunities for training at the institutional level, at the professional level, and in the craft skills for which the Islamic worker was so famous in the past.

Establishing the conservation course at Cairo University is a step in the right direction. What is needed, however, is a program of practical conservation techniques. The building industry needs to be supported and the EAO's own craft training program must be expanded to meet these challenges. Conservation is not just about building with craft skills applied to a modern frame. It is about caring for both the fabric and the spirit of the building. Do you like your historic buildings old or new? It is very easy to restore the building but to kill its spirit in process. Al-Hakim is a well known example of this in Cairo. Yet even here, after extensive reconstruction, loose parapet stones still threaten the lives of children playing beneath. Replacement technologies and the use of modern material must be treated with great caution. Modern technologies are part of our armory of weapons, but high-tech computer modeling and sophisticated photogrammetry do not mend monuments. Understanding how to employ the traditional skills in using lime and its special properties does.

Add to this the need to control the money. Whatever the source of funds, whether it is Egyptian money, whether it is foreign money, multilateral aid, bilateral aid, or private investment, it is critical that we avoid waste. We must establish procurement safeguards and responsible tendering procedures. That is not to say that we must always accept the lowest tender, but it does mean that tenderers must understand for what they are pricing. Terms of reference need to be drawn up carefully, specifications must be prepared. Simply to say that we are going to repair these monuments on the equivalent of a cost plus basis—that is, time and material plus a percentage for profit—is an immediate admission of failure. Equally vague tenders that call for lump-sum bids based on minimal information will be impossible to award in responsible manner. It is perfectly practical to specify in advance what works are necessary to the majority of these buildings. Clearly defined procedures are needed to ensure project control, which we as professionals have a responsibility to ensure are maintained.

The methods of contract and procurement need to be thought through to achieve the best quality results from a sensible budget. Clearly, speed is of the essence, so perhaps the usual path followed in submitting specifications, drawings, and tenders may be too slow for political purposes. So why not consider management construction or the American version of construction management? The slight subtleties need not concern us now, but what is essential is that the client takes the maximum advantage of the contractor's organizational experience, the architect's professional experience, and the archeologist's historical experience. We must ensure an unbiased, transparent, contract award procedure. This process needs to be clearly and responsibly organized from the inception of a project.

In Cairo we have an added complexity. We are working with monuments within a living city. This is not like dealing with a temple out in the desert; the community perception is critical to political success. We need to consider how buildings can be reused without compromising their historic or cultural integrity. The methods of public participation and community planning must be an important part of the conservation activity if the local public is to understand and appreciate the cultural importance of the city in which people live and work. Conservation in these areas is perhaps the most difficult task that the multi-professional team has to face. The key to success is to keep the projects discrete and small, at least to begin with.

The repair of the water and services infrastructure program in Cairo is progressing and it is understood that within the next four years the Fatimid city will have its service renewed. Some say that this causes more problems than it will solve. I think this debate will continue for years to come and well beyond the date of the new installation. What we do know is that in cities elsewhere in the world, the provision of modern services automatically brings with it an increased pace of development. As the favorable economic climate of that portion of a city changes, it becomes more attractive in terms of development opportunities.

This results in an increased loss of historic buildings. Sculptural and functional fragments can be disperrsed through the art market and there is a further erosion of the character of the city by the addition of poorly designed modern buildings. In historic Cairo, even the identification of all the historic buildings remains a basic need for ensuring adequate statutory protection.

We already know that the building control mechanism in historic Cairo does not work. You only have to walk through the city to see countless areas where the height regulations are flagrantly ignored, frequently by government buildings. Firm design control and strict building control are essential for new buildings. The monitoring of standards of repair to the historic buildings themselves is also essential.

Many of us have experience dealing with monuments in our home countries. From this we know that priority research is essential. We know the dangers of approving drawings that come in with details to match the existing structure written on the bottom, which the contractor is instructed to reproduce. Again it is a question of whether you like your historic buildings old or whether you prefer a reproduction that has lost the patina of time. Control is essential, with the need for regular inspection of all the works. There is need for the inspectors carrying out the control to have the authority to ensure that the materials, the detailing, and the design of the repair of the monuments in Cairo is to the highest possible standards.

Conservation architects nearly always support a cautious approach. Historic buildings should be repaired with traditional techniques and materials. The use of new materials must always be regarded with great suspicion. The work being undertaken today at the mosque of al-Aqmar is a good example of how things should not be done. This is not the conservation of a Fatimid mosque, it is the creation of a new building.

Phase one in the repair of the monuments in Cairo, the emergency propping, has now been done. But now what of phase two? The task before everybody is immense, and in many ways is perhaps best paralleled by the problem the Italians face in Venice. Unable to cope on their own, they have undertaken a program, with international support, spread out over twenty-five years and projected to the end of the next century.

Within Cairo it is clearly politically unacceptable to talk about a twenty-five year program to repair the monuments. Yet the opportunity exists to use the rapidly growing awareness of the theaters to Egypt's heritage for the EAO to transform itself into a management organization prepared and ready for the challenges of the next century.

But we must be careful not to go down in history with the buildings of historic Cairo appearing in the guidebooks as "reconstructed in the twentieth century." That would be an admission of our professional failure to conserve the best of the future.

Restoration Work in Cairo: Past, Present, and Future
Medhat al-Minabbawy

Restoration of Cairo's Islamic monuments has a long history. However, I will only try to summarize the accomplishments of the last twenty years in this field. In order to consider the future of restoration of Islamic monuments in Cairo, we must first reach back in history to the Comité de conservation des monuments de l'art arabe which was established on 12 December 1881 and later became a division of the Egyptian Antiquities Organization (EAO) known as the Islamic and Coptic Monuments section. The Comité made a survey of Islamic monuments in two maps and an index. It also kept a record of its restoration work and published it in what was called the Cahier de Comité. Altogether some forty volumes were published.

Foreign Missions in Islamic Cairo
The problems of restoration crystallized after the 1967 war. Having other priorities, the state did not deal effectively with the problem of funding and government trespassing on monuments. These difficulties remained unresolved into the early 1970s. In 1973, the Foreign Archaeological Institute was created to begin restoration in Islamic Cairo. The work would involve studies and research on monuments and excavations at historic sites.

The French Mission
The French mission was already working in the area under a cultural agreement with Egypt and was recording Islamic houses and palaces. This resulted in several studies of Islamic architecture in Cairo and proposals for restoration of a number of houses and palaces. The proposals included:
— the house of 'Abd al-Rahman al-Harawy (A.D. 1731)
— the house of al-Sitt Wasila (A.D. 1664)
— the palace of Alin Aq (A.D. 1293)
— palace of Amir Yashbak min Mahdi, palace of Qawsun (A.D. 1337)
— house–waqf Mahmud al-Shabshiri (A.D. seventeenth century)
— Qaʻa al-Ghanamiya (A.D. 1773)

The French Mission is currently restoring the house of 'Abd al-Rahman al-Harawy.

The German Mission

The German Mission is represented by the German Institute for Archaeology in Cairo (DAI) and operates in collaboration with the EAO. The DAI chose the Darb al-Qirmiz as a site for their activities. It contains:

— the mosque of Mithqal (A.D. 1367), restored
— the tomb of Shaykh Sinan (A.D. 1585)
— mausoleum and mosque of al-Higaziya (A.D. 1360), restored
— palace of Amir Bashtak (A.D. 1339), restored
— sabil–kuttab of 'Abd al-Rahman Katkhuda (A.D. 1744), restored
— madrasa of al-Kamil (A.D. 1752), restored
— mosque and mausoleum of al-Nasir Muhammad ibn Qalawun (A.D. 1304)
— mausoleum and madrasa of al-Salih Najm al-Din Ayyub (A.D. 1250)
— sabil–kuttab of Khusraw Pasha (A.D. 1535), restored
— minaret of al-Salih (A.D. 1343)

Some of the projects in the Darb al-Qirmiz were awarded Aga Khan restoration grants.

The Polish Mission

The Polish Mission has been working in the Mamluk cemetery in Cairo since 1972. In addition to numerous studies and excavations, the mission has restored:

— the complex of Amir Kabir Qurqumas (A.D. 1506)
— the complex of Sultan al-Ashraf Inal (A.D. 1460)

The Danish Mission

As a result of a cultural agreement between Egypt and the Danish government, the Bayt al-Sihaymi (A.D. 1648) and al-Gawhariya school attached to al-Azhar mosque were chosen for restoration by a group of professors from the Royal Danish Academy. The two buildings were studied and al-Gawhariya school was restored between 1980 and 1983.

The American Mission

The EAO approved the restoration of the Bayt al-Razzaz by the American Research Center in Egypt (ARCE) and studies were made with the EAO, but the restoration was never completed because of a lack of financial support.

The Italian Mission

The Italian Mission is represented by the Italian Cultural Center. The dome of the Mawlawi dervishes situated in the Mamluk burial site of Hasan Sadaqa was chosen for restoration. The Italian Mission requested permission to restore the sama'khana or the dervish theater. Architectural drawings were executed between 1977 and 1978 and restoration progressed through 1988. It was then agreed that a center for the training of architects, archaeologists, and restorers would be based in the Mawlawi lodge and that monuments on al-Suyufiya Street in al-Hilmiya al-Gadida would be restored.

The Bohari Mission

The Bohari Mission restored the Fatimid mosque of al-Hakim (A.D. 933–1013) and Qurqumas dome (A.D. 1011), which was moved from the entrance of the mosque to the Mamluk cemetery. They are currently restoring the mosque of al-Aqmar (A.D. 1125).

The EAO's Perspective

The activities of foreign missions led to increased media attention on the problems of restoring Islamic monuments in Cairo. Press coverage highlighted Cairo's neglected cultural heritage and resulted in enthusiastic international support to remedy the situation. The German Institute for Archaeology hosted an international seminar, in collaboration with the Goethe Institute and the EAO. This seminar, held from 1–5 October 1978, dealt with the preservation of historic architectural centers. The proceedings of the seminar were published in 1980. Representatives of twenty countries discussed the problems of Islamic Cairo and reviewed other examples of preservation throughout the world. The seminar resulted in an international call for the preservation of Islamic Cairo, and UNESCO, which had participated in the seminar, included Islamic Cairo in its World Heritage list.

The first international conference for the preservation of Islamic Cairo was held in 1980 to discuss the UNESCO report. This conference on the preservation of Islamic Cairo was held on the occasion of the one-hundredth anniversary of the French Institute. The first international conference recommended the founding of a maintenance agency in Cairo, which was called the Executive Organization for the Rehabilitation of Islamic and Fatimid Cairo.

Several recommendations rose out of the discussion at the First International Conference for the Preservation of Islamic Cairo. These included the implementation of a program to maintain and repair Islamic monuments while remaining sympathetic to local concerns. A request was made to place a five-year freeze on all current and planned construction and demolition, as well as on alterations to existing streets in Islamic Cairo. This freeze would permit time for initiating educational programs and ensure that all public and private rehabilitation was under the supervision of the proposed maintenance agency.

The conference also promoted a large-scale study of all legal matters—laws, regulations, administrative rules, and judicial decrees—pertaining to the preservation or demolition of historic buildings or the construction of new ones in Islamic Cairo. This step was to simplify and facilitate the resolution of social and economic problems as they relate to the development of the urban environment, particularly the issue of housing.

The conference encouraged the city government of Cairo to set up a committee to oversee new construction and to implement an education program on maintenance and repair. The members of this committee were to be experts from inside or outside the civil service. Further, it was mandated that all information concerning the maintenance and repair of Cairo's architectural heritage should be collected in one official document and that all restoration or preservation projects in Islamic Cairo should be registered and noted in this publication. Such a publication would ensure the protection of streets and monuments in Islamic Cairo. Finally, the conference stated that a review and examination of all historic buildings be done on a regular basis every five years.

The conference asserted that the main reasons for the dilapidation of the monuments and urban tissue of Islamic Cairo were: high population density; deficient maintenance of private property; escalating land values, leading to the price of property exceeding that of the buildings of it; demolition or collapse of buildings; insufficient funds for the care of Islamic monuments; rise in the underground water level and the faulty sewage network, leading to an increase in salts; lack of respect for our heritage; industrialization in and around historic sites; air pollution; and traffic intensity in the area.

From the EAO's point of view, the main tasks of the Cairo Maintenance Agency are: (1) to freeze for five years all construction permits for industrial purposes, new streets, or widening of old streets at historic sites; (2) to evacuate buildings undergoing restoration by the EAO; (3) to eliminate all trespassing on Islamic monuments.

The 12 October 1992 earthquake violently underscored the need to address all the problems identified in the various seminars and conferences. As a result, the EAO formed an executive service for the maintenance and restoration of Islamic and Coptic monuments on 25 October 1992.

There are many problems facing restoration of Cairo's Islamic monuments. The most important of these include: (1) trespassing by locals; (2) trespassing by governmental authority; (3) trespassing on surrounding areas; (4) lack of storage space for building materials in some monuments; (5) problems concerning electricity, water supply, or sewage systems; (6) problems of coordination with district officials concerning protective zones around the monuments. To solve these problems, it will be necessary for government entities to cooperate with each other and to collaborate with the EAO.

Bibliography

Association for the Urban Development of Islamic Cairo. *Preservation and Rehabilitation of Islamic Cairo: Some Background Papers.* Cairo, 1980.

Comité de conservation des monuments de l'art arabe. Exercice 1882–83. Cairo: Imprimerie nationale, 1898.

Dzierzykray-Rogalski, Tadeusz, and Medhat al-Minabbawy. "Burial Courtyard of Emir Qarbas Qasuk in Old Cairo." *Africana Bulletin* 35 (1988).

Dzierzykray-Rogalski, Tadeusz, Jerzy Kania, and Medhat al-Minabbawy. "The Investigation of Burial Crypts in the Mausoleum of Princess Tatar al-Higaziya in Cairo." *Annales islamologiques* 23 (1987).

Eighth International Congress of Turkish Art. Cairo: Ministry of Culture, Egyptian Antiquities Organization, 1987.

Fanfoni, Giusuppe. "Il complesso Architettonco de l'devisci mewlewi." *Rivista degli studi orientali* 57.

Godlewski, Wlodzimierz, ed. *Coptic Studies Acts of the Third International Congress of Coptic Studies, Warsaw, 20–25 August, 1984.* Warsaw: Panstwowe Wydawn. Nauk., 1990.

Grimal, Nicolas-Christophe, ed. *Prospection et sauvegarde des antiquités de l'Egypte.* Cairo: Institut français d'archéologie orientale du Caire, 1981.

Meinecke, Michael. *Die Restaurierung der Madrasa des Amirs Sabiq al-Din Mithqal al-Anuki und die Sanierung des Darb Qirmiz in Kairo.* Mainz am Rhein: P. von Zabern, 1980.

Meinecke, Michael, ed. *Islamic Cairo: Architectural Conservation and Urban Development of the Historic Centre.* London: Art and Archaeology Research Papers, 1980.

Misiorowski, Andrzej, et al. *Mausoleum of Qurqumas in Cairo: An Example of the Architecture and Building Art of Mamlouk Period.* 2 vols. Warsaw: PKZ, Polish–Egyptian Group for Restoration of Islamic Monuments, 1979.

Paolo, Cuneo. *Storia dell'urbanistica: il mondo islamico.* Rome: Laterza, 1986.

Polska Akademia Nauk: Travaux du Centre d'archéologie méditerranéene de l'Académie polonaise des sciences 28 (1990): pp. 240–81.

Revault, Jacques; and Bernard Maury. *Palais et maisons du Caire du XIVe au XVIII siécle.* Vol. 2. Cairo: Institut français d'archéologie orientale du Caire, 1977.

Wohlert, Vilhelm. *Restaurering i Cairo.* Nytaar: Kunstakademiets Arkitektskole, 1984.

The Egyptian–German Restoration of the Darb al-Qirmiz, Cairo

Philipp Speiser

Cairo has without doubt one of the largest number of Islamic, or to be more precise, Arab monuments of any Near Eastern city (fig. 1).[1] They are mainly located in the city center, the districts of Bulaq and Misr al-Qadima, in the northern and southern cemeteries, as well as on the island of Roda. How many monuments survive today remains unclear, as the last list of monuments, counting some five hundred buildings, was published back in 1951.[2] One might assume that over the last forty years, another one hundred monuments have either collapsed or have been demolished. In addition, there are an estimated five hundred buildings, most of them examples of domestic architecture, which were never listed.[3] It is therefore only a slight consolation that since 1951 new monuments have been registered, but their names have yet to be published.[4]

The ruinous state of most of those monuments has been deplored in countless publications. We owe the first critical descriptions to European travelers, who went to Egypt well before the French occupation of 1798. The French scientists collaborating in the *Description de l'Egypte* provided more accuracy, and furthermore, some engravings indicating neglected buildings.[5] Throughout the nineteenth century, Arab monuments, especially those in Cairo, remained in a sad state. Even the Khedive Isma'il was aware of the situation and in 1868 ordered the repainting of the outside of the chief monuments in alternating red and white stripes imitating a Mamluk tradition, in the hopes of giving the historic city a more pleasing appearance. One of the most vivid accounts was published by the French writer Arthur Rhoné, who deplored the rapid disappearance of monuments due to the Khedive Isma'il's modernization schemes of the 1870s.[6] In the twentieth century, especially in the last thirty years, the threat to Cairo's architectural heritage has become a major concern of scholars and journalists.[7]

It would be wrong to conclude from these statements that nothing has been done to save those buildings. As early as 1881 a conservation agency called the Comité de conservation des monuments de l'art arabe was established in Cairo, which was attached first to the Ministry of Religious Endowments *(awqaf)* and later to the Ministry of Public Education.[8] In 1953 the Comité was merged with the Egyptian Antiquities Organization (EAO). Forty volumes of yearly reports testify to the enormous work done by the Comité over a period of more than seventy years, and it is no doubt thanks to its efforts that so many of the listed monuments have survived. In 1953 the EAO took over from the Comité, and since 1981, efforts in conservation have been intensified. These nevertheless provide only partial solutions to the ongoing destruction of the historic urban fabric.

The main reasons for this state of affairs can be summed up as follows:

— The EAO has to act alone, since there is no formal collaboration with other authorities such as the governor, the city planning office, the building authorities, the public water and electricity board, etc.

— Some sources of destruction, such as a high water table or defective sewers, are beyond the scope of restoration schemes.

— Monuments and their surroundings receive only slight legal protection.

— The historic districts, although losing inhabitants, are subject to constant and often uncontrolled building activities intruding on protected sites.

— The EAO lacks multidisciplinary conservation units and therefore some of the restoration work is not of the best quality.

— Maintenance and monitoring of monuments is underdeveloped.

— With the exception of the Citadel, area-conservation has not been applied so far, that is, the single-monument approach is still very much in use.

— Restoration efforts tend to concentrate only on a certain number of larger buildings and the smaller structures, frequently located in back streets, tend to be overlooked.

More points could be added to this list. The idea however is not to criticize the efforts of the EAO but to make clear why things work differently in Egypt than in many other countries. To be fair, one has to say that in the historic districts of Cairo architectural elements have been preserved that exist nowhere else in the world, and for which conservationists are justifiably proud. Examples are the street patterns that closely resemble those recorded by the French around 1800, commercial activities that have been kept alive, and traditional lifestyles maintained. Also, Cairo has not succumbed to the fatal mistake of allowing historic buildings to be entirely refurbished internally as long as the façades are preserved.

Since 1973 the Egyptian restoration efforts have been assisted to a certain extent by foreign or joint missions. Beginning in 1971 experts of the Polish Center of Archaeology have been engaged in the restoration of the tomb of Qurqumas.[9] Between 1976 and 1987 the Italian Cultural Institute in Cairo undertook and completed the restoration of the dervish complex and is currently working on the Hasan Sadaqa madrasa attached to it.[10] In 1980–84 the School of Architecture of the Royal Danish Academy of Fine Arts worked on the madrasa of al-Ghuri annexed to al-Azhar mosque.[11] Probably the most controversial efforts have been made by the Boharis, a Muslim community from India, who since 1979 have "reconstructed" the mosque of al-Hakim and are currently completing the mosque of al-Aqmar. From 1983 to 1993 French experts supervised the restoration of the house of al-Harawy.[12]

The German Institute of Archaeology (DAI) has been working in the district of al-Gamaliyya since 1973.[13] The German restoration project can be divided in two phases. The first, completed in 1984, which concentrated on five monuments bordering on the Darb al-Qirmiz (figs. 2, 3), will be presented in detail. The second phase, which began in 1985, has completed four buildings[14] centering on a nearby section of the Shari' Mu'izz li-Din Allah, and a governmental grant has been awarded recently for a new project.[15] Giving advice is one thing, implementing it is another. It might therefore be worthwhile describing not only the restored buildings but to explain how the project was carried out and to review its advantages and weaknesses.

One of the first and most important decisions was the selection of a suitable restoration project. As mentioned before, all restoration efforts have previously been marked by the outdated single-monument approach, which concentrates on one building and tends to ignore its neighborhood. In order to avoid this, rather than selecting an isolated structure to restore, a small lane called the Darb al-Qirmiz in the Gamaliyya district was chosen. The lane branches off from the northern section of Shari' Mu'izz li-Din Allah halfway between Bab al-Futuh and the Khan al-Khalili bazaar. The Darb al-Qirmiz used to link Shari' Mu'izz and Shari' al-Gamaliyya.[16] The Darb al-Qirmiz features among its buildings five listed monuments (fig. 3): two Mamluk madrasas, one Mamluk palace, one Ottoman mausoleum, and one Ottoman sabil–kuttab. In restoring these five buildings, which can be seen as the cornerstones of the built fabric, the idea was to encourage the upkeep of the other buildings, mostly houses built within the last hundred years, or at least halt their decay. Bordering the Darb al-Qirmiz are also two empty sites for which reconstruction projects have been studied. The reason for concentrating efforts on listed monuments rather than unlisted buildings is quite simple: only the listed monuments are under the care of the EAO, and therefore speaking legally, public property. Providing funds for private property by a foreign institution would have been much more complicated, if not impossible.

The choice of an area rather than an individual building also meant that monuments were not selected only for their artistic value but also for their location. Added to this was the feeling that the restoration of monuments standing clustered together has a greater visual impact than restoration of buildings widely separated.

Project Management

From the beginning, it was clear that the most effective strategy for such an undertaking would be a joint venture with the EAO, allowing for a reduction of costs and true partnership. Therefore the DAI and the EAO each designated project leaders, who cooperated to outline the working program, the cost estimates, and a time schedule, basing themselves on a detailed survey of the actual state of each building.[17] These preliminary documents were then submitted to the EAO and the DAI respectively. In addition to the two institutions, further logistical and financial help was provided by the German Embassy and the German Academic Exchange Service (DAAD), both in Cairo.

The daily running of the site was again entrusted to the two project leaders, who were assisted by two site foremen on loan from the EAO.[18] This intimate linkage of the two institutions also allowed for greater flexibility when it came to decision-making. The original work program provided guidelines rather than a detailed schedule. This made it possible to adapt restoration work to unforeseen discoveries, and necessary changes could be made on the spot without time-consuming consultation of higher authorities. A very important condition for this kind of management was the almost daily presence on site of the project leaders and their availability at any time.

Craftsmen or Workforce

Initially a contractor was charged with the actual building work, but since a restoration is not a new construction, the necessary quality of work was not ensured and endless discussions on supplement payment for extra work threatened the project. It was therefore decided to hire all workers by day only—a decision that instantly brought much more satisfying results. A builder or mason and three to four laborers were almost constantly employed. They were joined temporarily by one or two carpenters, a group of plasterers, stone-carvers, electricians, and plumbers. The more specialized work, such as the restoration and completion of stucco or marble work, was entrusted to local experts. Conservation of timber and mural paintings were taken care of by restorers from the EAO or other institutions. Although the lack of skilled craftsmen and restorers is notorious in Cairo, the length of the project (which has already been twenty years) allowed for the training of gifted craftsmen in the field of restoration on the site itself. It was certainly an enormous asset to be able to work over a long period with the same people, people who knew their work and knew what quality was expected from them.

Restoration Techniques and Materials

Limited funds and the scarceness of sophisticated restoration equipment and materials on the local market, especially in the early years of the project, very much influenced the technical approach toward restoration work. It excluded any complicated techniques, which could have been executed by foreign specialists only. As a result, much more emphasis was put on the use of traditional building materials, such as red brick, stone, and timber, with the timber being mostly imported. Bonding and plastering was done mainly with mortars composed of slaked lime, sand, and the addition of crushed brick or timber ashes. Long-forgotten techniques were revived. For example, masonry covered by salt crystals was cleaned by applying layers of mud, new coats of plaster were reinforced with linen fibers, and brick walls were strengthened with horizontally inserted timber beams. Modern materials were only used for the restoration of decorative elements, especially painted woodwork, metal parts, marble mosaics, and stucco work.

Restoration Approach

With each building, great care was taken to preserve as much as possible of its historical substance, including later additions. There was no question of converting a building to its so-called original appearance, which, for want of precise historical records, remains speculation in any event for most structures. The only changes accepted concerned the installation of electricity, modern plumbing, and improved roofing, which were justified on the grounds that they helped to protect the historical remains and ensure their future use.

The completion of decorated elements was done very much along the same lines. Ottoman ceilings were therefore not replaced by Mamluk replicas, and a well-preserved nineteenth-century stucco window was not replaced simply because all the other windows in the room dated back to earlier centuries. The restoration of purely decorative parts was guided either by protective or by aesthetic considerations, e.g., the completion of a stucco frieze served effectively to protect the remaining original elements, the reconstruction of the marble mosaics of a prayer niche emphasized its importance for the worshipers. In order to avoid confusion between old and new, all recreated elements were clearly marked with a date.

Use of Monuments

Another vital question concerned the use of restored buildings. The Darb al-Qirmiz project was always based on the belief that daily use ensures to a certain degree at least continuing care and control. Therefore, the two madrasas were handed back to the Ministry of Religious Endowments and are now used for religious services. The sabil–kuttab, which could not resume its original use, was meant to serve as an information center for tourists with a little cafeteria on the upper floor, but is now used as a museum open to the public. The small mausoleum is also a museum. The palace, which is much too vast to be used for living, houses a permanent exhibition on the development of historic Cairo and the restoration project. It also displays copies of old engravings featuring Cairo and its monuments in the nineteenth century. In addition, concerts are performed in the big hall, especially during Ramadan. It is sad to note that the Ministry of Religious Endowments has not yet reinstalled the cult in the prayer hall or the Zawiyat al-Fijl located in the palace.

Funding

Funding for four projects was provided by the cultural section of the German Ministry of Foreign Affairs. In addition, the City of Hamburg sponsored the restoration of the sabil–kuttab of 'Abd al-Rahman Katkhuda. This money was administered by the DAI. The EAO contributed the loan of equipment, made material from governmental stores available, and rendered multiple services. It delegated certain members of its staff to help the project. By cooperating, the initial funds have been nearly doubled. Cooperation proved to be a great asset, making money immediately available with no wasted effort of negotiation before work could begin.

Impact on the District

One of the aims of the project was to revitalize the Darb al-Qirmiz quarter and to encourage owners of adjacent buildings to maintain them. These goals were only partly attained. Two buildings were repaired by the inhabitants and a third was pulled down and a commercial structure built in its place, probably based on the assumption that the restored monuments of the Darb al-Qirmiz would attract more tourists. Because of the permanent presence of a restoration team on the site, these building activities were closely monitored and the owners encouraged to respect building regulations. Still, many houses remain in urgent need of repair and basic improvements on the infrastructure, such as of the public water system, repaving of the streets, and new street lights would have gone well beyond the scope of the project. The inhabitants followed the restoration work with great sympathy and interest. The inauguration of each newly restored monument brought a festive mood to the district, and the presence of local and foreign politicians at these gatherings always led to the most welcome removal of large amount of debris and rubbish in the area.

Catalog of Restored Monuments in the Darb al-Qirmiz Quarter

Madrasa of Amir Mithqal al-Anuki
The madrasa of Amir Mithqal al-Anuki (Index no. 45) built in A.D. 1368–69/ A.H. 770 stands on a square site measuring little more than twenty by twenty meters.[19] It has one very elaborate street elevation (fig. 4) on the northern side made of limestone. The ground level of the madrasa contains storerooms, a water tank, and an internal staircase. It is divided into two parts by a vaulted public pathway. Its square plan is maintained on the first floor (fig. 5) by using the four-iwan concept of the Cairene madrasa with an open courtyard

at its center. The second floor contains a series of rooms, the former living quarters for teachers and students.

Work was begun in 1973 and lasted until 1976. The building itself was in a state of total neglect and had ceased to function as a mosque many decades before. The upper floors were in an advanced state of decay, the staircases and most of the ceilings had collapsed. For this reason the remaining structural parts were secured and the missing portions rebuilt. The roofs were fitted with a new waterproof surface, which is also easy to clean, and all walls except the main elevation were newly plastered. Missing decorative elements such as the stone crenellations and the lower part of the marble mosaic of the prayer niche were completed. Conservation work was only applied to the carved wooden ceilings and the stucco windows. New decorative additions were the marble floor of the courtyard and the wooden pulpit.[20]

In 1976 the building resumed its new function as a mosque. The Mithqal madrasa served as a pilot project in every respect, from the site management to the appropriate restoration technique of marble fragments. Although some procedures have since been modified and updated, the concept as a whole has remained unchanged over the last two decades.

Mausoleum of Shaykh Sinan

The mausoleum of Shaykh Sinan (Index no. 41) dates from A.D. 1585–86/A.H. 994 and represents one of the earliest Ottoman buildings in Cairo.[21] The structure occupies one of the angles of the Darb al-Qirmiz and is erected on a very small and nearly rectangular site (fig. 6). The building is covered by two domes. It looks very small from the outside, partly because it is half sunk into the ground because of a more than one-meter rise in the street level since the sixteenth century. The height and division of the roof by twin domes gives the interior a surprisingly spacious quality. Except for the brick domes, which are covered by plaster on the outside and stucco ornaments on inside, the mausoleum is built entirely of limestone.

In addition to the usual work on the structure and the decorative elements, the original entrance, which had been blocked by rubble, was reopened and made accessible by a new flight of steps.[22] The interior was freed from an ugly coat of blue paint left from the time when the building was used for housing, and a new floor pavement was laid out. The wooden cenotaph received a new green cover and electric glass lamps were installed.

Madrasa of Tatar al-Higaziya

The madrasa of the Princess Tatar al-Higaziya (Index no. 36) is situated on the 'Atfat al-Qaffasin, which connects Midan Bayt al-Qadi with Shari' al-Gamaliyya.[23] The irregularly shaped building is centered on an open court-yard with two iwans (fig. 7), one on the east and a larger one on the south side. The north side shows a triple arcade supported by reused columns of Byzantine origin. The minaret, of which the top has been missing since the nineteenth century, lies south of this arcade. Access to the madrasa is provided by a corridor from the north. The mausoleum, covered by a dome made of stone, is situated in the northern corner of the building (fig. 8). The ablution court lies in the western backyard. The madrasa's external elevations, including the minaret, are entirely built of limestone, while inside brick is used for the upper floors. The building displays fine stucco work (fig. 9) in an inscription frieze running along the courtyard, in the iwans as well as in the arcaded room. A series of niches set in the upper section of the courtyard and the semidomes of two mihrabs are also made of stucco. The high quality of craftsmanship shown here is matched by three carved and painted wooden ceilings.[24]

The building was erected in two phases. In A.D. 1347/A.H. 748 Princess Tatar, daughter of Sultan al-Nasir Muhammad, built the mausoleum for her recently murdered husband. The tomb was most likely an extension of her palace. The palace itself was converted into the madrasa in A.D. 1360/A.H. 761. This largely explains the irregular plan of the building.

Restoration work on the building required two years, from 1980 to 1982. Apart from the repair work on the structure, including the securing of the leaking roofs, the completion of floors, and the plastering of all internal walls, considerable effort was put into the conservation and completion of the decorative elements. I would like to highlight a few of these elements.

Missing sections of the inscription frieze mentioned above were completed with the help of a graphic designer from the EAO[25] and the extraordinary skills of the stucco artist.[26] The repetitive ornaments were reproduced by casts, whereas the calligraphy and its interlaced floral decor were carved by the artist on the wall itself. In order to gain a regular depth of carving, two slightly different colored layers of gypsum were applied. Missing stucco niches in the courtyard were copied from the existing ones, and the stucco grilles of the mausoleum's four windows were also restored and the colored glass completed. As in the madrasa of Amir Mithqal, the carved ceilings were only cleaned and their painted surface consolidated but not completed. All timber elements such as the minbar,[27] doors, window grilles, cupboards, and so forth were restored. The marble decoration of the main mihrab was temporarily removed, cleaned, and completed.[28] The mosaics of the cenotaph in the mausoleum were only cleaned and strengthened.[29]

Sabil–Kuttab of 'Abd al-Rahman Katkhuda

The sabil–kuttab (fountain and school-house) of 'Abd al-Raman Katkhuda (Index no. 21) dating from A.D. 1744–45/A.H. 1157 is probably one of Cairo's most famous and most widely depicted Ottoman building (fig. 10).[30] Its fame owes as much to its architecture as to its prominent location in the middle of the historic main street, exactly at the point where the Darb al-Qirmiz branches off. The sabil–kuttab, built on a square plan, is two floors high. The exterior of the building displays very elaborate stone carvings and marble mosaics. Below street level there is a large water tank (fig. 11). The ground floor consists of a spacious room with water basins on three sides allowing passersby to help themselves to water. It features a remarkable tile revetment of Istanbuli origin and a painted ceiling. The upper floor consists of a loggia-like schoolroom, which is decorated with ornamented woodwork including another painted ceiling. Attached to these rooms are the former living quarters of the teacher and the guard. Unfortunately these living quarters have never been listed and are therefore are not eligible for restoration.

Funds provided by the City of Hamburg made it possible to start work in 1980, which was completed in 1984. The building itself showed traces of decay almost everywhere. Most affected were the timber roofs, which had to be dismantled and rebuilt. Similar work had to be done on the internal staircase and the floor of the schoolroom. The decorated ceilings were cleaned and consolidated. The trickiest part proved to be the completion of the tile revetment, of which the lower parts had been destroyed by salt corrosion. After several fruitless efforts to produce the tiles locally, a manufacturer in Kütahiya was contracted and eventually produced the replicas.[31]

Palace of Amir Bashtak al-Nasiri and the Zawiyat al-Fijl
The only secular listed monument bordering the Darb al-Qirmiz is the palace of Amir Bashtak al-Nasiri (Index no. 34) built in A.D. 1335/A.H. 736–1339/ 740.[32] The large size of the structure shows in the dimensions of the elevation facing the main street (fig. 12), of which the lower part is built in limestone and the upper part in red brick covered by plaster. Its ground floor contains several vaulted storage and service rooms, as well as a prayer hall, the Zawiyat al-Fijl, and a series of shops. The upper floors, of which only some parts have survived, are taken up by a huge reception hall with two iwans and two lateral arcades topped by a harem gallery (fig. 13). Adjacent to the big hall, several smaller rooms have been preserved. Although restored in the 1930s (but never finished), the entire structure was, with a few exceptions, in a decayed state. Restoration work lasted from 1982 to 1984. At first, efforts concentrated on the structural parts. Some decayed sections were removed and rebuilt and others strengthened. Later the roofs and staircases were reconstructed, blocked windows and doors were reopened, and the floors newly paved. As one part of the upper floor did not show any traces of the original rooms, it was decided to convert it into a large terrace rather than creating a fancy ruin.33 After those basic interventions, the interiors of the main rooms, including the entrance hall, the storage rooms, the reception hall and its adjacent rooms were restored. In all of them new door leaves were inserted, missing window grilles completed, and ceilings and vaults restored. In the great hall, a new marble fountain was installed and all the stucco windows repaired.

Most of the external walls were replastered. This included even those of the unlisted buildings surrounding the courtyard of the palace. The initial project to lower the courtyard ground level, which over six centuries had risen by one and a half meters, had to be limited to the area around the entrance gate.[34] In contrast to the other projects, the restoration of the palace of Bashtak al-Nasiri did not lead to its complete overhaul. Nonetheless, it provides the visitor with a sequence of rooms, including the Zawiyat al-Fijl, which evoke the building's former splendor.

Although operating with a modest infrastructure and on low budgets, the DAI and the EAO have together restored not less than nine buildings and work has just started on the tenth. What is even more important is the uninterrupted sequence of activities in two adjacent areas. They have firmly planted the idea of restoration in the district of al-Gamaliyya, improved restoration methods, and trained numerous local craftsmen. The project also attracts a steady flow of visitors, who otherwise would never have ventured into that historic area.

As has been said before, this kind of project can neither deal with nor solve all the problems in this particular area. It would, for instance, have been desirable to have the area improved on all levels. But at least no one can seriously argue that the buildings are not worth being preserved, or that the preservation of monuments is impossible in Cairo.

The least satisfying aspect is probably the maintenance of restored monuments. Although all buildings are being used and cleaned daily, the passing of a broom over floors is not sufficient for their upkeep, and the extensive use of buckets of water is rather harmful.[35] All buildings, especially old ones, require thorough maintenance: roofs have to be cleaned, plaster has to be patched up, woodwork treated, broken pavements refitted, light bulbs replaced, drainage pipes cleared, broken windows replaced, and so on. Experience shows that these activities are beyond the of capacity of the ordinary watchmen or the cleaners employed by the EAO. Therefore it is absolutely necessary to establish a well-equipped maintenance service with an adequate budget, which is as efficient as the one employed by the Cairo Metro. In the long run, regular inspection of the monuments and maintenance would greatly reduce the costs of restoration work.

Notes

1. According to *The Egyptian Antiquities Law* no. 117 (1983), buildings erected one hundred years or more ago are eligible for the list of monuments.
2. *Survey of Egypt,* "Map of Cairo Showing Mohammedan Monuments" [in 1:5000] (Cairo, 1950), sheets 1 and 2; *Survey of Egypt,* "Index to Mohammedan Monuments in Cairo," 1951 (reprint. Cairo: The American University Press, 1980).
3. This was demonstrated by Viktoria Meinecke-Berg and Michael Meinecke, "Preliminary Report on the UNESCO Survey of al-Jamaliyya," in Michael Meinecke, ed., *Islamic Cairo: Architectural Conservation and Urban Development of the Historic Center, Art and Archaeology Research Papers* (June 1980), pp. 30–34.
4. It would be of great help if updated lists of monuments were regularly published, as had been done until 1951.

5. *Description de l'Egypte*²—planches: état moderne I (Paris, 1822), pl. 15–72; Edmé François Jomard, "Explication du plan du ville du Caire et de la citadelle," *Description de l'Egypte*²—texte: état moderne XVIII/2 (Paris, 1829), pp. 134–288.

6. Arthur Rhoné, "Coup d'oeil sur l'état présent du Caire ancien et moderne," *Gazette des Beaux Arts* 24 (1881): 420–32; 25 (1882): 55–67, 144–53.

7. For the most balanced views on this topic see Meinecke, *Islamic Cairo*; Caroline Williams, "Endangered Legacy" *Middle East Journal* 39 (1985): 231–47.

8. On the history of the Comité see Philipp Speiser, "Dei Geschichte der Erhaltung islamischer Bauten in Ägypten seit 1882" (Heidelberg, forthcoming).

9. See Ireneusz Nieduziak, "Polish–Egyptian Restoration Work at the Burial Complex of Amir Qurqumas," in Meinecke, *Islamic Cairo*, pp. 47–51.

10. See Giuseppe Fanfoni and Carla M. Burri, "The Mawlawiya and the Madrasa of Sunqur al-Sadi with the Mausoleum of Hasan Sadaqa," in Meinecke, *Islamic Cairo*, pp. 62–65; Giuseppe Fanfoni, *Il restauro del Sama Khana dei Dervisci Mevlevi* (Cairo, 1988).

11. See Vilhelm Wohlert, "An Egyptian Danish Restoration Project," in Meinecke, *Islamic Cairo*, pp. 66–72.

12. Bernard Maury, "Dix années d'activités, Palais et maisons du Caire, la maison Harawi," in *Observatoire urbain du Caire contemporain*, Lettre d'information no. 19 (Dec. 1989), pp. 8–12.

13. Michael Meinecke, "The Darb Qirmiz Project," In *Islamic Cairo*, pp. 42–46; Michael Meinecke, "Die Restaurierung der Madrasa des Amirs Sabiq al-Din Mitqal al-Anuki und die Sanierung des Darb Qirmiz in Kairo," *Archäologische Veröffentlichungen* 29 (Mainz, 1980), pp. 87–119, Pls. 39–41b; Sherban Cantacuzino, ed., "The Darb Qirmiz Quarter," in *Architecture in Continuity, Building in the Islamic World* (New York, 1985), pp. 94–101; Philipp Speiser, "Dix années d'activités: Institut allemand d'archéologie du Caire," in *Observatoire urbain*, Lettre d'information no. 22–23 (Dec. 1990), pp. 11–15.

14. The following buildings were included: madrasa of al-Kamil (Index no. 428), madrasa of al-Nasir Muhammad (Index no. 44), mausoleum of Sultan al-Salih Najm al-Din Ayyub (Index no. 38), sabil–kuttab of Khusraw Pasha (Index no. 52).

15. On the most recent projects, see Nairy Hampikian's article in this book.

16. The Darb al-Qirmiz is blocked halfway by a structure built at the turn of this century.

17. The EAO entrusted the direction of the work to Muhammad Fahmy and Medhat al-Minabbawy, and the DAI appointed Michael Meinecke from 1973 to 1977, Philipp Speiser from 1979 to 1988 and Nairy Hampikian since 1989, as project leaders.

18. Saad al-Habal and 'Abd al-Fadil Awad.

19. See Meinecke, "Die Restaurierung der Madrasa Mitqal," pp. 29–79, 140–44, pls. 1–32, 44a–c.

20. The pulpit contains several old elements secured in one of the stores of the EAO.
21. Meinecke, "Die Restaurierung der Madrasa Mitqal," pp. 79–86, pls. 33–36.
22. This allowed for the elimination of an emergency door.
23. Philipp Speiser, "Restaurierungsarbeiten in der islamischen Altstadt Kairos," in *Mitteilungen des Deutschen Archäologischen Institutes Abteilung Kairo*, vol. 38 (1982), pp. 363–78, pls. 76–86.
24. They cover two iwans and the entrance room.
25. Muhammad Rushdy.
26. Ibrahim 'Abd al-Munhim.
27. The present is a crude nineteenth-century replica of the Mamluk original now on display in the Islamic Museum.
28. The completion was inspired by the mihrab of the nearby madrasa of Gamal al-Din al-Ustadar.
29. This work was carried out by Michel Wüttmann from the IFAO.
30. Meinecke, *Die Restaurierung der Madrasa Mitqal*, pp. 79–86, pls. 33–36.
31. Metin Cini Company.
32. See Philipp Speiser, "La Restauration du Palais Bastak," in *L'habitat traditionnel das les pays musulmans autour de la Méditeranée*, vol. 3 (Cairo, 1990), pp. 810–26, pls. 233–44.
33. This section of the palace was demolished around 1900 when a new house was erected in its place. The upper floors of that house have since collapsed.
34. If the level of the courtyard had been lowered everywhere, it would have been flooded whenever a sewer was blocked in the neighborhood.
35. For example, in the sabil–kuttab this has led to severe damage of the tile revetment.

Fig. 1. The Citadel and its surroundings, ca. 1880 (after E. Béchard and A. Palmieri).

Fig. 2. General view of the Darb al-Qirmiz and its surroundings: (21) sabil–kuttab and house of 'Abd al-Rahman Katkhuda; (34), palace of Bashtak al-Nasiri with Zawiyat al-Fijl; (36), madarasa of Tatar al-Higaziya; (41), mausoleum of Shaykh Sinan; (45), madarasa of Mithqal al-Anuki.

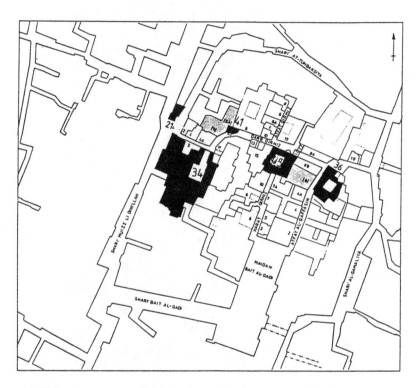

21 Sabil–kuttab and house of 'Abd al-Rahman Katkhuda 41 Mausoleum of Shaykh Sinan
34 Palace of Bashtak al-Nasiri with Zawiyat al-Fijl   45 Madrasa of Mithqal al-Anuki
36 Madrasa of Tatar al-Higaziya

Fig. 3. Location of restored monuments in the Darb al-Qirmiz.

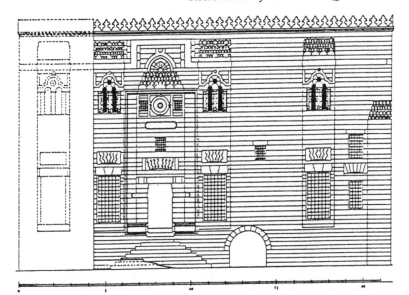

Fig. 4. Main elevation of the madrasa of Mithqal al-Anuki (drawing by Galal M. Ali).

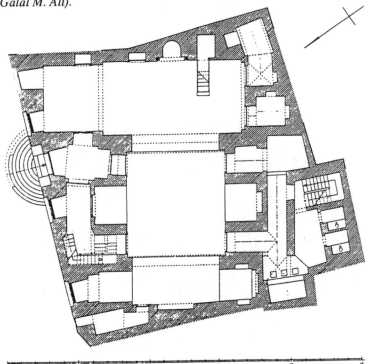

Fig. 5. First-floor plan of the madrasa of Mithqal al-Anuki (drawing by Galal M. Ali and S. Melbinger).

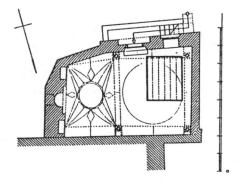

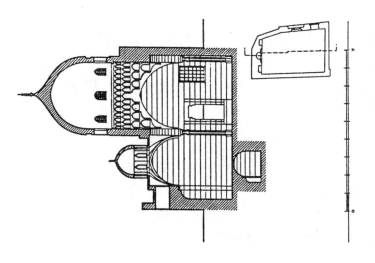

Fig. 6. Section and ground plan of the Mausoleum of Shaykh Sinan (drawing by Galal M. Ali).

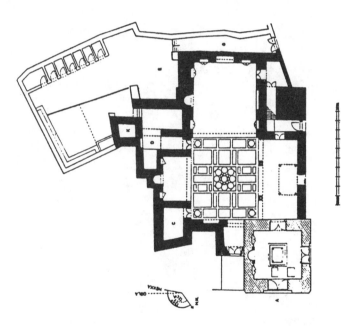

Fig. 7. Ground-floor plan of the madrasa of Tatar al-Higaziya.

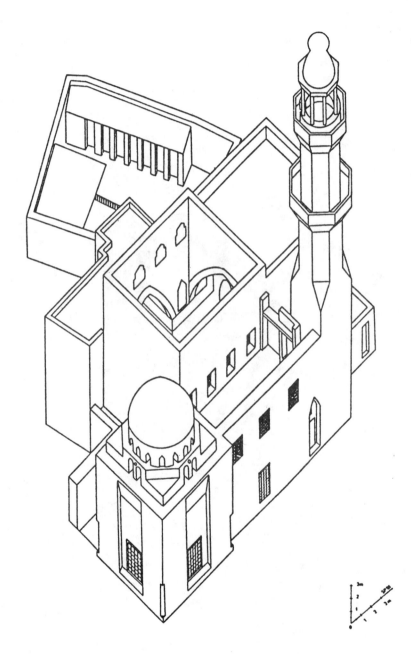

Fig. 8. Isometric view of the madrasa of Tatar al-Higaziya.

Fig. 9. Main iwan of the madrasa of Tatar al-Higaziya.

Fig. 10. Sabil–kuttab and house of 'Abd al-Rahman Katkhuda.

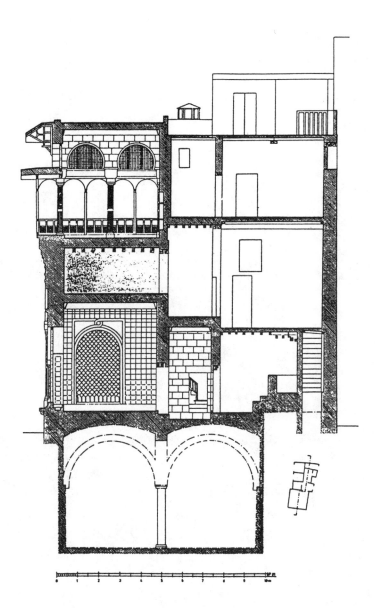

Fig. 11. Longitudinal section of the sabil–kuttab and house of 'Abd al-Rahman Katkhuda.

Fig. 12. Main elevation of the palace of Bashtak al-Nasiri.

Fig. 13. Large reception hall in the palace of Bashtak al-Nasiri.

Restoration of the Mausoleum of al-Salih Najm al-Din Ayyub

Nairy Hampikian

On the spine of al-Qahira, the Fatimid addition to the 1,353-year-old Islamic capital of Egypt, in the heart of Shari' al-Mu'izz, in the area still called Bayn al-Qasrayn (between the two palaces), stands the mausoleum of al-Salih Najm al-Din Ayyub (fig. 1).[1]

During the last fifty years, the rising water table, the deteriorating sewage system, lack of maintenance, modern transportation in the old city, erection of new, ugly, and unstable high rise buildings, as well as many other factors have accelerated the breakdown of Islamic monuments. Since 1973, these, and a wide range of criteria, have been taken into consideration when selecting monuments to be restored by the German Institute of Archaeology in Cairo in collaboration with the Egyptian Antiquities Organization.

The program included restoration of one monument followed by a chain of others, resulting in the revitalization of one whole street by restoring all its monuments, then moving on to another neighboring street, and so on. The ultimate aim is to take the first steps toward the revival of a whole district. The arena of the restoration projects was intentionally centered in the heart of the medieval city, al-Gamaliyya, on the ground formerly occupied by the great Fatimid palaces—an area with the highest density of monuments within historic Cairo. By 1990, the German–Egyptian rescue program had already completed the restoration of seven monuments when it started its eighth project. This was the restoration of the mausoleum of al-Salih Najm al-Din Ayyub. The project was underwritten by a grant from the City of Stuttgart and its mayor, Manfrid Rommel.

Najm al-Din Ayyub became sultan in 1240. During the second year of his reign, he built his madrasa on the site of the eastern Fatimid palace, after having part of it demolished. In 1249, he died in al-Mansura fighting the crusaders under the command of St. Louis IX. This is where the role of the wise Shagar al-Durr (tree of pearls) appears. As the widow of the sultan, she decided with some faithful friends to keep the sultan's death a secret until the arrival of Turan Shah, the son of al-Salih, who was in Hisn Kayfa, on the Tigris. With much secrecy, she sailed up the Nile in a small boat to the castle of Roda where she hid the corpse of the sultan. She handled all the affairs of state until the departure of the Franks when she announced the death of Sultan al-Salih Najm al-Din Ayyub. When Turan Shah was murdered, she declared herself sultana over all Egypt. Her short reign was unique in Islamic history since it was a woman who became the ruler, minted coins, and had her name mentioned at Friday prayers in all the mosques. Besides running the state, she pulled down the great hall reserved for the shaykh of the Malikis of al-Salih's madrasas and instead erected an attractive mausoleum for her deceased husband. The historian al-Maqrizi (A.D. 1364–1442) describes the official burial ceremony:

> The people came out on Friday to the castle of al-Roda from where the body of the sultan was borne. They prayed over him after the Friday prayer. All the soldiers wore white and the Mamluks shaved their hair. Condolences were received and the sultan was buried that night. For three days all the markets in Cairo and Egypt were closed. The burial ceremony was performed with tamborines in Bayn al-Qasrayn. Consolation was received until Monday.[2]

Much political insight and intelligence was needed to introduce a royal tomb inside the city—and not just anywhere, but on the very site of the eastern Fatimid palace just across Shari' al-Mu'izz—the street once known as the processional pathway of the Shi'ite Fatimids. Shagar al-Durr quite cleverly continued her husband's tactics of eliminating the Fatimid presence from the city by demolishing their political centers (their two palaces). Moreover, she tried to distract the attention of the public from the Shi'ite shrines of the Fatimids, which were outside the city gates. She made a new political declaration, which was most welcomed and followed by her successors—Baybars al-Bunduqdari, Qalawun, al-Nasir Muhammad, and Barquq. By then the Fatimid palaces had completely disappeared, without leaving trace, as they were replaced by a political, institutional, and memorial center of a new dynasty—that of the Mamluks. (Nevertheless, even today that part of Shari' al-Mu'izz is stilled called Bayn al-Qasrayn, referring to the two Fatimid palaces).

Having thrown light on the personality of the sultan buried in the mausoleum, the character of Shagar al-Durr who built it, and the historical context behind the erection of the building, we will make a close analysis of the restoration project.

The Façade and its Problems

The façade on the right side of the entrance follows the style of the still-existing madrasa of al-Salih using similar keel-arch panels with shell-motif hoods. Three of these are on the western façade and one on the southern. The architect has broken the alignment of the façade of the madrasa by projecting his construction outward into the street. This has given his building a new dimension and created a wider angle of visibility to the dome. The same scheme was used in the madrasa of al-Zahir, which was, in turn, built one step further into the street than the mausoleum of al-Salih. Of all the existing examples, these three once-monumental buildings, built one after the other and in proximity to each other, exhibit the same solution to an architectural problem. Later, the frequent use of this type of relation between new and existing buildings added the dimension of architectural surprise to the city of Cairo. At the beginning of this century, shops were built right across the façade of the mausoleum and people lived on its roof. Actually, with the exception of the interior of the mausoleum, the whole monument was inhabited. The picture taken from the nineteenth volume of the Cahier de Comité published in 1906 clarifies the situation. Fortunately, the Comité evacuated the roof and the façade of the mausoleum and demolished all the invading structures.

An examination of the façade revealed the twin problems threatening all Cairene monuments—the rising ground-water table and the overloaded sewage system. The obvious solution would seem to be the lowering of the water table and an overhaul of the sewage system in the whole of the old city. The Egyptian government is now exerting every effort to fix the sewage system. It is interesting to emphasize here that already the first phase of the sewage project executed by the Egyptian government outside the city gates—at the eastern side of Bab al-Nasr—has had its effect on some of the most critical spots within the historical core of the city. The street in front of the mausoleum suffered severe inundations every other day. To reach the site, one had to use the balcony of the neighboring house. Since the completion of the first phase of the sewage project, the area is spared from daily assaults of sewage water. Nevertheless, the problem has still not been completely solved. In the meantime, restoration projects should have contingency plans in place for these problems, as both the rising water table and inadequate drainage of sewage water cause the corrosion of the lower fabric of the buildings and consequently the weakening of the core of their walls.

On closer examination, we noticed that blocks replaced during previous restorations were more sensitive to saline corrosion, the body of the mortar by which previous restorations were done was not suitable, and that the Comité used very thin layers of mortar between the blocks, which caused these to suffer minor vertical cracks. The cracks are superficial, running only on the facing blocks but never inside the core. These observations highlighted the defects of previous restoration techniques that needed to be avoided.

The humidity problem was handled by allowing the maximum aeration of the lower fabric of the walls. This does not eliminate the existence of water, but reduces to a minimum its capillary action through the walls. First, we analyzed the mortar in different areas of the building and used only the original mortar ingredients. Then we dug a trench one meter wide with a depth of one and a half meters around the internal and external walls of the mausoleum (whenever it was possible) and filled it with gravel. We also created an auxiliary system of horizontal passages through the whole width of the wall, in some spots allowing the free passage of air. Finally, we replaced blocks affected by saline corrosion. Other areas were isolated by different methods, such as the wall behind the mihrab, the mihrab proper, the burial chamber, the central wooden cenotaph, and the horizontal external platforms of the transitional zone open to the sky. After carefully analyzing the plaster on the external face of the dome, its composition was determined and a new plaster was applied matching as closely as possible that used in the thirteenth century.

The other restorations done on the façade are considered normal procedures, such as the conservation of the wooden windows, the iron grilles, the carved details of the lintels, and the restoration and completion of the crenellations and the decorative frieze under it crowning the uppermost part of the façade. On examination of the decoration on the frieze, it was obvious that parts of it had already been restored by the Comité. The missing blocks of the crenellation were completed by our stone masons.

Secondary Parts of the Project

The cross-vaulted entrance hall, measuring 3.40 by 4.35 meters, the partially destroyed tunnel-vaulted rectangular vestibule, measuring 3.60 by 5.78 meters, the outermost court (once the southern iwan of the madrasa of al-Zahir), and the vault of the L-shaped passage, which once led directly to the courtyard of the northern twin iwans of the madrasa of al-Salih, were restored, completed, and plastered (fig. 2). When the steps of the staircase leading to the roof were restored, it was discovered they were recycled pharaonic blocks bearing hieroglyphics. These were documented, replaced by replicas, and the originals sent to the stores of the EAO.

On removing the rubble blocking the L-shaped passage in order to aerate the wall behind the mihrab, nineteenth-century dishes, plates, pipes, a gas-lamp bulb, bank accounts, and letters were found, as well as newspapers such as *al-Ahram*, *al-Waqa'i'*, and *al-Muqattam* dating back to the 1890s. The date corresponds exactly with the Comité's report of 1893 concerning the evacuation of the people living "on the dome" and demolition of the encroaching structures added to accommodate them. Apparently, the passage had not been not cleared since that date. Suddenly we stumbled upon modern wooden beams. On investigation, it proved to be the ceiling of an extension to a coppersmith's shop next to the iwan of the madrasa of al-Salih. This was a completely unexpected intrusion. The owner had used a part of the passage in such a way as to be completely unnoticed from the exterior. With the help of local authorities and the EAO, the merchant was evicted from that part of the passage.

The Interior of the Mausoleum

The vast interior of the mausoleum (10.65 meters square) is surmounted by a dome with the help of a transitional zone composed of three tiers of stalactites, which appear in this building for the first time in Egypt. A set of three hexagonal stucco windows interrupt the transitional zone. As in almost all Cairene Islamic monuments, it is set askew to achieve the correct orientation of the qibla. In the case under review, this fact resulted in a difference in the thickness of the façade wall, measured through the windows, varying between 1.97 meters and 5.30 meters (fig. 3).

Once the structural condition of the dome was investigated, the cracks on the stone masonry, some parts of the internal core of the walls, and the stone blocks were treated. The plastering process started again only after specimens of the original plaster used for the various parts of the interior were analyzed to ensure once more that the components and mixture of the newly applied plaster were as close as possible to the original layer.

The transitional zone of the mausoleum includes three tiers of stalactites interrupted by four sets of stucco windows. The three original windows of the southeast wall, as well as the uppermost windows of the three other sides, needed restoration. We also replaced the central double windows of the three other sides by new ones, made by traditional methods still practiced in Cairo. The latter had been replaced during previous restorations by lattices pierced with circular holes. Five of the original windows were sent to the museum, while the sixth is exhibited in the interior of the mausoleum.

When the two layers of plaster applied during the previous restorations were removed, a light, pale blue brush paint appeared on the original layer of the stalactite zone and on the blind windows. Following the traces, it was possible to discern at least an outline of the designs. This is not surprising as the same area in the mausoleum of Shagar al-Durr bears similar motifs.

We discovered yet another new important piece of evidence that helped us restore the original appearance of the monument. Fragments of marble remains were found in situ on the lower parts of the walls, which attest to the encasement of the walls in marble, at least up to the height of the first wooden inscriptional frieze. We added new marble pieces, matching the color on each discovered fragment, to give an impression of the original texture.

On excavating the area under the wooden cenotaph, it was found that six limestone steps led through an arched opening to a rectangular tunnel-vaulted room (3.00 m. by 2.00 m.). A beautiful Naskhi inscription in pale blue, with an average width of 14 cm., was applied freely on the white plaster depicting verses from the Qur'an. It is one of the earliest surviving Naskhi scripts painted on a wall. On the qibla direction, traces of a mihrab were found. Because of the underground water problem and the deteriorating plaster, the endangered inscription was carefully removed and restored. We then planted it in wooden boxes filled with pure gypsum. The burial area was then consolidated, filled with sand and slate, and closed. The marble flooring of the mausoleum was also restored, guided by the traces of the original design.

Excavations were carried out under the marble floor of the interior of the mausoleum, in the outermost court, and in the passage leading to the madrasa of al-Salih. In all three excavation sites, remains of the northern wing of the madrasa of al-Salih, remains of the eastern Fatimid palace, pottery, and carved blocks of the madrasa of al-Zahir were found. Because of the paucity of archaeological evidence, very little is known for certain about the famous Fatimid palaces. Therefore these finds are of considerable importance.

Fine Restoration Work

These finds include all the wooden fragments, the upper inscriptional frieze, and the magnificently carved wooden cenotaph (fig. 5). The lower inscriptional frieze had been almost completely restored by the EAO before we started our work on the site. The cenotaph, measuring 2.33 meters by 1.30 meters and 1.30 meters high, has on its four sides Ayyubid star shapes and inscriptions running around the sides of each face. The date of the sultan's death is mentioned on the southern side. Dismantling the pieces gave us the opportunity to analyze and study the back faces of the cenotaph where we found unsuccessful attempts and reused carvings of earlier periods. The cenotaph was previously quite badly restored by the application of colors. Retreatment showed that the geometric patterns were emphasized only by the use of three kinds of wood naturally different in color—a splendid example of thirteenth-century Islamic woodwork.

The mihrab, the earliest existing in Egypt with a marble lining, was reconstructed using all the original marble pieces available and completely isolated from all possible sources of humidity (figs. 6, 7). Close examination of the decorated band on the mihrab showed the pattern to be broken. Obviously, the fallen pieces had been replaced haphazardly without following their original design. We were able to assemble scattered remains of that band (some were used face-down as floor slabs) and arrange them in their original sequence recapturing the original details. Apparently, the scrolls running along the band were filled with two different motifs set alternatively—a single composite-type flower and a group of three small flowers. The scrolls are separated from each other by a cuplike plant arranged in upward and downward directions. This is yet another fragment of the heretofore lost history of the thirteenth-century decorative arts.

After removal of the modern gold revetment on the four marble bases and capitals of the engraved dark-green marble columns of the mihrab, the finely carved floral details and the inscription running on all four sides bore witness that these were Fatimid pieces, probably from the eastern Fatimid palace.

With the restoration of the mausoleum of al-Salih Najm al-Din, the German Archaeological Institute has added its eighth link in the chain of restored Islamic monuments in the district of al-Gamaliyya. We hope that the great sultan and his wife Shagar al-Durr are satisfied with the efforts done to revive the mausoleum. Meanwhile, again with a grant from the city of Stuttgart, a ninth monument was saved—the sabil–kuttab of Khusraw Pasha built in 1535. Moreover, after the earthquake that struck Cairo on 12 October 1992, the Cultural Department of the German Foreign Affairs has made the decision to sponsor the consolidation and preservation of yet another unique monument in the same district—the minaret of the madrasa of al-Salih, which will be the tenth German–Egyptian restoration project.

If one takes into consideration the time needed to correct the sewage system, inflation rates, the dilapidated state of Islamic monuments, and the new damage after the earthquake, we realize that time is the strongest opponent in the struggle to preserve Egypt's Islamic heritage. Thus, even with the limited funds available, a strategy must be agreed upon that will ensure protection for all the indexed monuments. But, as for undertaking complete conservation, some priorities must be set that would systematically direct effort and resources.

Notes

1. Monuments restored by the German Institute of Archaeology in Cairo with the collaboration of the EAO from 1973 to 1990 are the mosque of Amir Mithqal (A.D. 1367), tomb of Shaykh Sinan (A.D. 1585), the madrasa and mausoleum of Tatar al-Higaziya (A.D. 1360), the palace of Amir Bashtak (A.D. 1334–39), the sabil–kuttab of 'Abd al-Rahman Katkhuda (A.D. 1744), part of the madrasa of al-Kamil (A.D. 1752), and the minaret and tomb of al-Nasir Muhammad (A.D. 1296–1304). These monuments were restored under the direction of Michael Meinecke and Philipp Speiser, while the eighth project—the mausoleum of al-Salih Najm al-Din Ayyub—was carried out by myself.

2. Al-Maqrizi, *Kitab al-Suluk*, 1–ii, p. 371.

Fig. 1. Overhead view of the mausoleum of al-Salih Najm al-Din Ayyub.

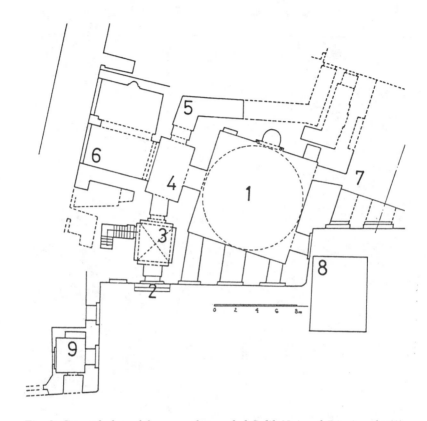

Fig. 2. Ground plan of the mausoleum of al-Salih Najm al-Din Ayyub: (1) mausoleum; (2) entrance; (3) cross-vaulted entrance hall; (4) vestibule; (5) L-shaped passage; (6) outermost court; (7) remains of the madrasa of al-Salih; (8) sabil–kuttab of Khusraw Pasha; (9) remains of the madrasa of al-Zahir.

Fig. 3. Sectional isometric of the mausolem of al-Salih Najm al-Din Ayyub.

Fig. 4. Interior of the mausoleum of al-Salih Najm al-Din Ayyub.

Fig. 5. Northern face of the cenotaph.

Fig. 7. Mihrab after restoration.

Fig. 6. Mihrab before restoration.

The Italian–Egyptian Restoration Center's Work in the Mevlevi Complex in Cairo

Giuseppe Fanfoni

The Italian–Egyptian Restoration Center (C.F.P.R.) was inaugurated in 1988. On this occasion, the restored sama'khana of the Mevlevi dervishes (a well-known Turkish order) was opened to the public and to visitors. The restored sama'khana is part of a large architectural complex in which the Italian–Egyptian Restoration Center is located. It is responsible for the recovery of other historic buildings in collaboration with the Egyptian Antiquities Organization. It also serves as a training center for Egyptian restorers of the EAO and students of Egyptian universities, and has been sustained since 1977 with contributions from the Italian Ministry of Foreign Affairs.

The Architectural Complex

The area, which is at the foot of the Citadel, comprises buildings of different ages and purpose. The planimetrical, historical, and archaeological study undertaken shows that the most ancient buildings were architecturally connected by the Mevlevi dervishes in the course of the last intervention (between the seventeenth and nineteenth centuries). The most imposing part of the complex is the so-called Yazbak Palace on the east side of the area (built and enlarged in the time of Qawsun, Yazbak, and Aqbardi between the fourteenth and fifteenth centuries). The mausoleum of Hasan Sadaqa, the minaret, and the remains of the madrasa of Sunqur Sa'di (partially reused for the building of the Mevlevi sama'khana) engage the west side of the complex, fronting Shari' al-Suyufiya (fig. 1). The whole area was given to the Mevlevi dervishes in 1607 by Prince Sinan, and they, in various phases, adapted the existing buildings to the needs of the confraternity.

They built a new wing on Shari' al-Suyufiya, which allowed access to the large Aqbardi garden and to the conventional area. Then they built the eighteen cells of the convent around the garden, where the internal front of the sama'khana is located, and around the Aqbardi garden, largely preserving the existing structure of the Yazbak Palace (figs. 2, 3). At present, handicraft laboratories have been set up in the area of the convent for various specialized sectors devoted to restoration (woodwork, metalwork, ceramics, drawing, photography, etc.).

Methodology of Intervention

A historical study of the buildings of the area has been carried out on the base of a planimetric survey of the whole architectural complex. At the same time, both a technical survey of the sama'khana and the first urgent intentions to save the collapsing dome were undertaken. The gradual acquisition of historical and technical data during the course of the first restoring operations made the complexity of the restoration project more and more evident and interesting.

The cognitive and operative aspects of the problem of this monumental restoration are interlinked. The technical study of the complex (implying surveys and inquiries) is useful for gaining information on the historical period as well as on the typological character of the buildings, but at the same time it gives us information on the techniques and materials used, which is necessary for deciding how to carry out the project with respect to the historical data. Until now, the main restoration has focused on the sama'khana, the Hasan Sadaqa mausoleum, and the Sunqur Sa'di madrasa (where the restoration is in progress).

The Mevlevi sama'khana is a cultural domed building built on a central plan, mostly of wood and reusing such ancient structures as perimetrical walls. In fact, it was built on the space of the main court of the Sunqur Sa'di madrasa and on the walls surrounding it, but at a level three meters higher than the original. The main problem we faced was to restore the sama'khana and at the same time carry out archaeological excavations under it, keeping the underlying structures (figs. 4, 5).

The urgency of the work coupled with the wide variety of technically and historically interesting aspects impelled us to start the recovery project in 1979 with the aim of rescuing the sama'khana and the underlying archaeological remains. An analytical study of the ancient techniques revealed the use of very low-level technology and poor materials, which caused static trouble to the monument as soon as it was built.

It is a problem that more or less concerns most of the Islamic monuments in Egypt. We have confronted it by studying and applying appropriate technologies, which have integrated the original and local techniques, and have maintained the functionality of the building while preserving the aesthetic and formal aspects of the monument. Advanced technology, with the use of particular machinery imported especially from Italy, is now being applied to stop the rising humidity in the Hasan Sadaqa mausoleum. This is an operation that does not interfere with the general methodological lines, but develops them further. It is in fact the only way that has been found to solve the problem. Moreover, it may be applied to any Egyptian monument.

Restoration Techniques

The restoration operations were defined as the result of the technical surveys and studies made for the restoration itself (cracks of the structure, settlement and crevices, out of plumb, etc.) on the buildings to the east of the architectural complex. The areas of restoration concerned: consolidation of the walls; consolidation of the wooden dome of the sama'khana; archaeological digs of the Sunqur Sa'di madrasa around and under the sama'khana; temporary work supporting the structures during the time necessary for the completion of the digs; new foundations of the internal structures of the sama'khana; restoration of the wooden beams and reinforcement of the floors to meet maximum safety loads; some seismic retrofits of the structures; tempera painting restoration; interruption of rising moisture in the walls of the sama'khana using resin injections and the realization of air space for ventilation; and interruption of rising moisture in the walls of the Hasan Sadaqa mausoleum by cutting the walls through the whole thickness and inserting a waterproofing layer.

Strengthening the Walls

The masonry of some parts of the walls has completely deteriorated because of the constant infiltration of polluted water and the formation of salts produced by rising moisture. In other parts, settling of the foundations created cracks and empty spaces in the wall structures.

We consolidated the stone walls with injections of a mixture of lime and powdered inerts similar to the original mortar, with the addition of acrylic resins, in order to achieve reinforcement in a shorter time. In addition, the brick walls on the south side, belonging to the Sunqur Sa'di madrasa, have been strengthened by a mixture of epoxy-resins allowing better capillary penetration of the material in the numerous cracks and internal crevices that have occurred over time.

Care has been taken to preserve the visible traces of the functional, artistic, or formal changes in the history and reuse of the building; a graphic representation on the north and east external plaster shows us the presence and situation of more ancient structures inside. On the south, the reused brick wall of the Sunqur Sa'di madrasa, has been left without plastering in order to testify to different periods of construction (fig. 6).

Restoration of the Dome

When we started restoration work in the area, the sama'khana dome was in danger of falling down as it had been flattened and distorted by a great deal of settling of the foundation. After supporting the dome from the inside with wooden scaffolding, we applied a steel belt on the outside (composed of three elements) at its reins. By tightening the hoops gradually and checking the reduction of the cracks from inside, the dome recovered as far as possible its original shape with a rising of twelve centimeters in the top. The wood centers were strengthened by epoxy-resins and some of them were replaced. The laths forming a covering under and over them were sewn up with strips of wire netting. Glass wool was put inside the hollow spaces for thermal insulation. A lime mortar, quite similar to the old one in its composition, with the addition of acrylic resins, was applied to the outer surfaces (fig. 7). A movable panel on the extrados allows us to see the restoration work carried out inside the dome section.

Archaeological Excavations

The digs under and around the sama'khana were done with the twofold aim of locating points of static settlement (all the pilasters were out of plumb [see fig. 8]) and of studying the ancient underlying structures. Stratigraphic excavations of the archaeological and architectural remains were carried out. With this information, we decided to hang up pilasters to bridges supporting the two-level floors of the sama'khana and the load of the dome in the affected areas.

After the conclusion of the archaeological excavations in the court of the Sunqur Sa'di madrasa, we laid a foundation in the area below the ground level. The ancient wood pilasters were resettled to plumb with a saddling mechanism and extended with iron pilasters discharging the load on the new foundation plinths. Then they were linked together as well as to the four perimetrical walls by an horizontal iron structure which is the definitive floor of the sama'khana and, at the same time, allows one to visit the excavated ancient remains.

Completion of the structure took a long time but the problems we faced have been largely rewarded by the historical interest of the findings and the importance of the architectural remains relating to the Tulunid and earlier periods. Their publication is in progress.

Structural Consolidation of the Floors

The second floor, which consists of a circular balcony looking down on the performance area, has been strengthened according to calculations for the safety load (see fig. 9, scheme B). The roof has been made 50 percent lighter by removing heavy and useless materials and restructured by laying a glass-wool coat as thermal insulation. The corners and the floor of the structure have been strengthened in accordance with public safety standards. The original appearance of these areas has remained unaltered (fig. 10). All the wood has been treated with disinfectant and preventive substances with a base of pentachlorophenol and a final coat of Paraloid B72.

Seismic Retrofits of the Sama'khana Structures

The seismic retrofit of the building structures is integrated into the restoration projects: a perimetrical concrete beam is fitted inside the thickness of the wall, linking the wooden structure of the roof and the dome with the vertical walls. The shape of the roof square has been strengthened by diagonal iron tie-bars anchored to the concrete beam (fig. 5).

Moreover, the new iron floor linking the perimetrical walls constitutes an anti-seismic connection at the ground floor level of the sama'khana. New careful connections of all the joints of the wooden structure and the strengthening of the walls with injections are an improvement of the structure that helped save the monument during the October 1992 earthquakes.

Restoration of the Paintings

The dome paintings, retouched and altered many times and darkened by sediments of dirt, were reduced to scales, and, in some points, these had fallen, leaving gaps. Firstly, the scales were wetted and reattached to the walls by spraying resins (Paraloid B72, 5 percent).

A study of the original paintings and the following restorations and repairs was carried out using ultraviolet shots and analyses of microscopic sections. Based on this, we had a fairly clear picture of how the paintings originally appeared and evolved as they were retouched and repainted.

Originally the sama'khana was simply painted in white and ivory yellow, with red and blue squares. The dome was white and illuminated by eight windows (the number eight has a special mystic symbolism in the Mevlevi ideology). The most interesting phase in the dome is the period of the tempera landscape (Turkish Rococo). During that period the dome windows were closed. In order to keep the paintings and to make it possible to see the dome in the original light, we installed eight simultaneously movable window panes (fig. 3).

During the same period when the landscape paintings were done, ancient doors of the madrasa on the ground floor had been walled up and covered from inside the sama'khana by wooden panels. Oval windows were opened in order to provide a soft light. We have installed a double frame system, which has allowed us to open new doors (complying with the present safety standards for public places and corresponding to the ancient madrasa doors) and to keep the beautiful panels with the oval windows (fig. 8).

As for the paintings on the dome, the period in which the landscapes were done has been retained since this era has the most complete documentation. The sky of the landscapes was sprayed by a velatura of Parloid B72 and natural pigments. The paint is easily reversible and does not interact with the layers underneath. The velatura neither dims the view of the tonal variations, nor the surface consistency of the dome, nor even the traces of the restored cracks reminiscent of the history and vicissitudes of the building.

Elimination of Moisture in the Walls

It is well known that the chief factor in the decay of all Egyptian monuments is moisture. The problem is particularly prominent in the buildings fronting Shari' al-Suyufiya, both for the alluvial ground and for the great quantity of polluted water in the area.

In the sama'khana, we have carried out a series of combined works for this purpose. Two rows of holes, made in alternate position and spanning the thickness of the masonry under the level of the floor, have been filled with injections of epoxy-resins in order to reduce the suction on sections of the walls.

A one-meter-wide air space was excavated around the sama'khana beneath the level of the outside pavement; it was later covered, leaving two openings on the north and the south in order to provide continuous ventilation, which effectively solves the problem (fig. 6).

Different types of binders have been selected for the restoration of the internal paintings and for the paint used on the outside. These allow a transpiration movement on the outside surface, thus keeping the internal decorations. Five years later, no water lines have appeared on the walls. The capillary suction of water from the ground is the main factor causing the decay of the mausoleum of Hasan Sadaqa and the adjoining liwan of the madrasa, the buildings where we are presently working.

The disintegration here is caused, as in many Egyptian monuments, by the presence of various water-soluble salts, chiefly sodium chloride. The rising water dissolves and brings the salts to the surface, where they crystallize and cause external pulverization and internal swelling, ultimately leading to spot destruction or even the total collapse of structures.

The particular techniques employed in the sama'khana would not be effective in this part of the complex, where the water level is presently and constantly at a few centimeters underground. In this case, we have resorted to advanced technology to create a physical block against the water present in the foundations.

We are using special machinery made in Italy (donated by Ansaldo) to cut through the entire thickness of the walls. It is a hydraulic dry-operating piece of equipment, which avoids the use of water so dangerous in ancient and decayed structures. It works with a blade two meters long, but we are making another much longer one of special steel alloy.

For every twenty to thirty centimeters cut through the wall, strips of PVC are inserted into the void. At the same time a special mixture of expansion-controlled and sulfate-proof ferric cement without chlorides (donated by Pagel Italiana) is injected under them. The PVC strips have a special shape presenting grooves. Because of these, the mortar binds the upper and lower sides of the wall. This layer also strengthens the structure against seismic activity as confirmed on the occasion of the recent earthquakes (fig. 10). The technical precision of the operation allows the possibility of the removal of the layer with the same machinery used for inserting it, should this become necessary later.

Beginning in 1988, study (aided by funds from the Italian Research Council) has been done on the rising moisture from ground water, in which periodic measurements on a grid of fifty centimeters were done. Satisfactory results from this work support my hope that this new restoration technique may solve a problem suffered by most of Egyptian monuments.

Bibliography

Bongrani, L.; G. Fanfoni. "For an Executive Project of the Sphinx Archaeological Conservation." *Seventh International Congress on Deterioration and Conservation of Stone.* Lisbon, Portugal, 15–18 June 1992, vol. 3, pp. 1553–63.

Fanfoni, G. "Il restauro della Sama'Khana del Dervisci Mevlevi." Cairo, 1988.

————. "Il complesso architettonico del Dervisci Mevlevi in Cairo." *Rivista degli studi orientali* 52 (1983): 77–92.

Giordano, G., *Costruzioni in Legno.* Milano: Hoepli, 1964.

Lucas, A. *Disintegration and Preservation of Building Stones in Egypt.* Cairo: Government Press, 1915.

Massari, G. I. *Risanamento del locali umidi.* Milano: Hoepli, 1974.

Mastrodicasa, S. *Dissesti statici delle strutture edilizie.* Milano: Hoepli, 1974.

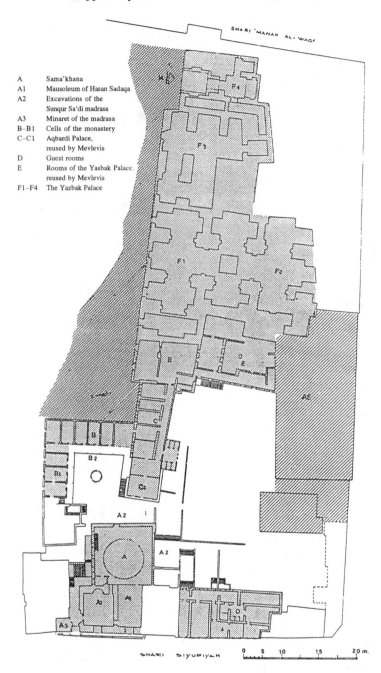

A   Sama'khana
A1   Mausoleum of Hasan Sadaqa
A2   Excavations of the
       Sunqur Sa'di madrasa
A3   Minaret of the madrasa
B–B1 Cells of the monastery
C–C1 Aqbardi Palace,
       reused by Mevlevis
D   Guest rooms
E   Rooms of the Yasbak Palace,
       reused by Mevlevis
F1–F4 The Yazbak Palace

Fig. 1. General plan of the Mevlevi complex, Cairo.

Fig. 2. Exterior of the sama'khana.

Fig. 3. Interior of the sama'khana.

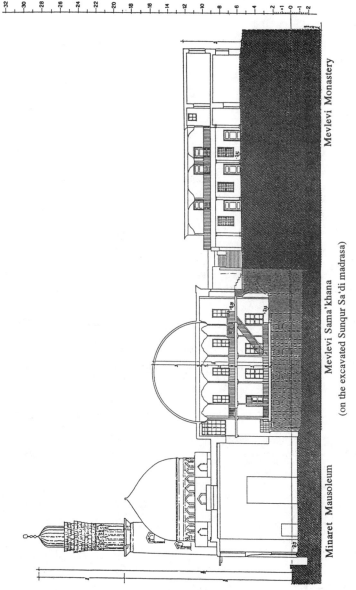

Minaret   Mausoleum   Mevlevi Sama'khana   Mevlevi Monastery
                       (on the excavated Sunqur Sa'di madrasa)

Fig. 4. Elevation and underlying structures of the sama'khana.

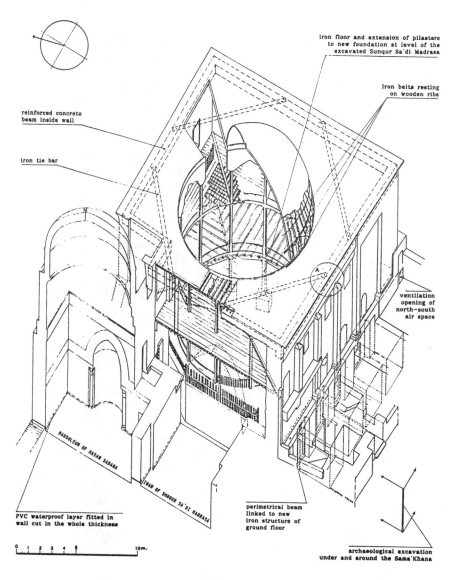

iron floor and extension of pilasters
to new foundation at level of the
excavated Sunqur Sa'di Madrasa

iron belts resting
on wooden ribs

reinforced concrete
beam inside wall

iron tie bar

ventilation
opening of
north-south
air space

MAUSOLEUM OF HASAN SADAQA

IWAN OF SUNQUR SA'DI MADRASA

PVC waterproof layer fitted in
wall cut in the whole thickness

perimetrical beam
linked to new
iron structure of
ground floor

archaeological excavation
under and around the Sama'Khana

0 1 2 3 4 5   10m.

Fig. 5. General scheme of the restoration work done at the sama'khana.

Graphic Representation of Previous Uses of Wall

injections of lime and powdered inerts

*injections of epoxy-resins
air space for north–south ventilation*

Elimination of Rising Damp from sama'khana

*Reused brick walls showing architectural elements of the
Sunqur Sa'di madrasa (windows, doors)*

Fig. 6. Masonry restoration and ventilation at the Sunqur Sa'di madrasa.

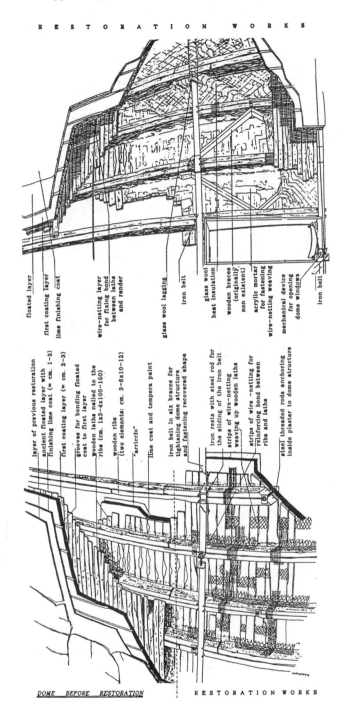

Fig. 7. Structural analysis of the restoration of the dome of the sama'khana.

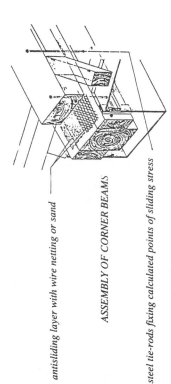

antisliding layer with wire netting or sand

ASSEMBLY OF CORNER BEAMS

steel tie-rods fixing calculated points of sliding stress

AFTER RESTORATION: The auxiliary doors system keeping the old wooden panels and including the oval windows.

BEFORE RESTORATION: Pilasters out of plumb (nos. 5, 6, 7); the wood panels, damaged by dampness, have been structurally reinforced and reused.

Fig. 8. Restoration of wood at the sama'khana.

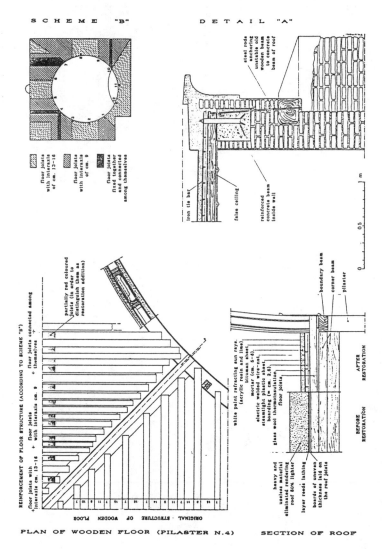

Fig. 9. Structural consolidation of floors at the sama'khana.

*detail of cutting
showing PVC layer
and filling mortar*

south wall, six months after cutting

*line of rising damp
(up to 5 m. with
90–95 percent humidity)*

Fig. 10. Elimination of rising damp at the mausoleum of Hasan Sadaqa.

A Polish–Egyptian Restoration Project at the Eastern Cemetery in Cairo

Jaroslaw Dobrowolski

The funerary complexes of Sultan al-Ashraf Inal and Amir Kabir Qurqumas, both outstanding examples of the architecture of the Circassian Mamluk period, are located in the northern part of Cairo's medieval necropolis, though designated as the Eastern Cemetery. For a long time, the area was mistakenly called the Cemetery of the Caliphs (as for example, David Roberts in his 1839 drawing of the area) and only recently has the far more appropriate name, the Mamluks' Desert, come into use. Paradoxically, this name is rapidly becoming inadequate as the area changes its character from a deserted cemetery to an urban district.

Excavations recently carried out by the Polish–Egyptian mission have revealed that the area was not as deserted as was presumed. The foundations of huge buildings apparently predating Inal's and Qurqumas' complexes were excavated. Both Sultan Inal's and Amir Qurqumas' foundations formed large multifunctional religious–funerary complexes of the kind quite typical and popular in Mamluk Cairo. While in most other instances these once-vast establishments were reduced to isolated tombs or mosques, in this case they have been preserved fairly complete, though much ruined and stripped of their originally lavish decoration. Both comprise a domed mausoleum built over a set of crypts, a mosque–madrasa with a minaret, a sabil (with a kuttab in the case of Amir Qurqumas), ablution courts, khankahs for sufis, a founder's residential premises (in the form of a finely decorated qa'a in Inal's and of a two-chambered residential wing elevated over an arcade in Qurqumas' complex), arcaded courts for less important burials, as well as service installations. Elaborate and sophisticated water-supply and sewage-disposal systems were in use. In both cases a crucial part of the complex was the mosque, built in the form of a typical Cairene cruciform madrasa. It has not been determined whether these were actually used for teaching.

The first to be erected was the complex of Sultan al-Ashraf Inal, built in several stages between A.D 1451 and 1456. A domed mausoleum was constructed when the founder was still an amir, a fact that may explain it being a little out of scale compared to the rest of the quite monumental complex that was erected after Inal had become a sultan.

The complex of Amir Kabir Qurqumas, the army commander of Sultan Qansuh al-Ghuri, was built directly adjoining to the south in the beginning of the sixteenth century. The domed tomb and madrasa were completed in A.D 1506. In 1509 a khankah connected the complex to Sultan Inal's buildings creating an unbroken—though quite diverse—façade spanning over two hundred meters along the street. The amir had chosen the site because of his admiration for Sultan Inal's edifice and this may explain the conservative aspect of his buildings. Their architectural forms, although undoubtedly of the highest quality, are rather somber and display none of the architectural follies fashionable in Sultan al-Ghuri's times. On the other hand, there is a striking similarity to the funerary complex of Sultan Qaytbay. This was built about thirty years earlier when Qurqumas (then Qaytbay's mamluk) was in his prime and embarking on a brilliant career. This suggests that the founder's own taste and personal preferences had a decisive influence on the building's form.

Both complexes were deserted probably soon after the Ottoman conquest, and later on were used as military barracks and depots. In 1883, they were returned to the waqf authorities and some restorations were done by the Comité de conservation des monuments de l'art arabe between 1913–19 and again between 1940–53, but the site continued to be used by the military and police, who only withdrew after the Egyptian Antiquities Organization's repeated requests.

In 1972 a Polish–Egyptian group was formed with the aim of restoring Amir Kabir Qurqumas' complex. Later the scope of the work was extended to include Sultan Inal's complex. The project was organized and sponsored on the Egyptian side by the Egyptian Antiquities Organization and on the Polish side by the PKZ, a state-owned company for monument restoration, and the Polish Archaeological Center of Warsaw University.

Although restoration was the main task of the mission, its activities were never confined merely to construction. Studies were done on historical sources, including the amir's foundation deed. The buildings were thoroughly examined, measured, and documented, including photogrammetric documentation. Comparative studies were also done on contemporary monuments. Anthropological examinations were performed on bone remains, rendering valuable information, including interesting paleopathological observations. Excavations were carried out in and around the buildings, and they revealed interesting and unexpected information, especially on the use of the site prior to the construction of the funerary complexes, and on late occupational phases.

As far as actual restoration is concerned, it was of prime importance to stop further deterioration of the site. This involved ending improper use of the premises. Although this was a long and painstaking process both in legal and technical terms, the site has been cleared of all previous users, put under the Egyptian Antiquities Organization's authority, and fenced.

The restoration work concentrated on ruined parts of Amir Qurqumas' mosque, tomb, and palace, with the aim of recreating a complete roofed building that could in the future be practically and safely used. Ruined parts of walls were rebuilt, including the fleur-de-lys cresting. The minaret was also thoroughly restored, including reconstruction of the top part with a finial and balustrades of the balconies. Missing ceilings were reconstructed throughout the complex. New roofs were installed over original ceilings in the madrasa, their design permitting future conservation of decorated wooden parts that were seriously damaged. Marble dado decoration was partly reconstructed in the madrasa's eastern iwan, after a thorough study of comparable contemporary material and archaeological examination of the remaining pieces. The interiors have been protected against unwanted visitors by installing window grilles, shutters, and doors.

In the complex of Sultan al-Ashraf Inal, thick layers of debris were an obstacle to any conservation. Large quantities have been removed but the task is far from finished and with current financial regulations within the Egyptian Antiquities Organization effectively blocking the use of appropriated funds, there is little chance that it can be completed in the next few years. The restoration in this complex so far amounts to refacing eroded walls.

All these works were designed and supervised by the Polish–Egyptian mission, which also supplied well-trained specialists for more difficult jobs, while most of the on-site construction work was done by Egyptian contracting firms. Since 1992 the mission has been reorganized; the PKZ company has withdrawn from the project, and on the Polish side, the Polish Archaeological Center in Cairo took full responsibility. In the season that followed, the system of contracting the works was abandoned and the Egyptian Antiquities Organization carried out the work directly.

The beginning of this season coincided with the powerful earthquake of 12 October 1992. The Polish Center immediately provided a preliminary report on the state of the monuments under its responsibility and was assigned to assess the damage in the whole area of the Eastern Cemetery. A report on the state of the area's thirty-five-odd monuments was presented to the Egyptian Antiquities Organization on 26 October 1992. It was stated that in most cases the damage was minor. In many monuments, however, the seismic shocks aggravated structural deficiencies that had been present before. Gypsum control marks were placed over cracks in endangered places and they were regularly monitored afterwards. The results were reassuring: the marks were found intact. However, the inspection made after the earthquake proved that most of the monuments in the area are in dire need of prompt restoration, with their cracked domes and walls, deformed arches, and rotting roofs.

A separate problem was the damage caused by the earthquake to the top stories of the four Mamluk minarets featuring colonnaded pavilions on top. Their monolithic marble columns have been broken at the base, making the structures extremely vulnerable to future earthquakes or strong winds. The tops of the minarets were temporarily shored up with timber by the Polish Center's team and provided with materials and manpower by the Egyptian Antiquities Organization, and the possibilities of more long-term treatment have been studied.

The future course of action for Amir Kabir Qurqumas and Sultan Inal's complexes is envisaged as (1) completing the restoration of the amir's mosque–madrasa and attached compounds and (2) protecting the ruined parts of the complexes against further damage and rendering them safe for visitors, while keeping the intervention into the original structures to the minimum necessitated by safety. This implies that any reconstruction of missing parts of the edifices should be ruled out, and also (contrary to a presently popular trend) that the idea of planting a garden around the complexes that originally stood in a desert setting must not be entertained. Exposition of archaeological remnants revealed by the excavations is envisaged instead.

The Preservation and Retrofit of Islamic Monuments in Cairo after the Earthquake of 12 October 1992

David W. Look

Cairo has an incredible wealth of Islamic monuments from all periods and styles. This has been recognized internationally by the designation of medieval Cairo as a World Heritage District. These highly significant resources are threatened and may be lost in the not-so-distant future if action is not taken to protect, stabilize, and eventually restore them.

The moderate earthquake of 12 October 1992, was a wakeup call to remind us that these resources are vulnerable to tremendous forces, which destroy and kill without warning. Earthquakes do not kill people; falling debris from buildings and/or collapsing sections of buildings kill people. As Sir Bernard Feilden has stated in his book *Between Two Earthquakes*, "we are always between two earthquakes," except, of course, for the few seconds of an actual seismic event. What should we do between now and the next earthquake to retrofit our historic resources? Experience has shown that seismic retrofitting unreinforced masonry buildings will not only save our cultural resources but also hundreds or thousands of lives.

The recorded history of the seismically active areas of North America is less than five hundred years, a very short period in geological time. Recorded history in North Africa and the Middle East is several thousand years old and documents the occurrence of earthquakes. The infrequent nature of earth-quakes has lulled us into a false sense of security. The earth's surface is made up of a number of large plates that have been shifting slowly for millions of years and undoubtedly will continue to do so in the future. Cairo is located close to the edge of the African Continental Plate.

Any historic resource located in an active earthquake is subject to the slow deterioration associated with the normal weathering of materials and the sudden damage from earthquakes, tsunami (if close to a body of water), and other disasters such as fires, floods, and high winds. In addition to these causes of destruction, the monuments of Cairo have been subjected to years of deferred maintenance, severe air pollution, and rising damp. Taken together, the cumulative adverse effect from all of these causes of deterioration and damage is staggering.

Once the downward spiral of less and less maintenance begins, it seems to be neverending. In general, as the cleanliness and maintenance of a religious site decreases, the site receives fewer and fewer people at prayertime and fewer tourists. As fewer worshipers and tourists visit the site, the site receives even less maintenance. Eventually, for safety and economic reasons, the site is closed to the public. Once closed, the site receives no maintenance, and deterioration progresses rapidly, eventually leading to progressive collapse. The abandoned site is frequently entered by vandals and/or occupied by squatters. Homeless people will often start fires to cook and to keep warm. They use whatever combustible materials they can find. Often these are pieces of wood from collapsed ceilings and roofs. Once these pieces are consumed by deterioration and/or fire, the evidence for the accurate reconstruction of these monuments is lost forever. This eliminates the possibility of salvaging pieces of original or early materials and craftsmanship. In general, deferred maintenance costs at least three times as much as routine maintenance.

For example, if a roof is not repaired or replaced when necessary, the leaking roofing will cause the roof sheathing and framing members to deteriorate. The leaking roof usually causes damage to other materials below such a plaster, woodwork, metalwork, and even stone. When one adds up the expense of repairing and replacing all these materials in addition to the expense of the roofing, the cost is great. The more time that elapses, the more costly the remedial work becomes. The figure of deferred maintenance costing three times as much as routine maintenance is based on experience in America where delays are only five to ten years at most. In areas where maintenance is deferred for decades, the cost is greatly increased and may be tens to hundreds of times as expensive. No cost figure can be placed on the loss of original design and craftsmanship. Not only does the integrity of the site decrease with passing time, but the site's structural capacity to resist gravity and lateral loads greatly diminishes. A decayed wooden structural member has only a fraction of its original capacity to support vertical loads and resist horizontal loads.

As the overall population of the Greater Cairo area has increased rapidly, the actual population of the medieval area of old Cairo has decreased. The lack of maintenance of residential structures has caused the abandonment of the upper stories of these buildings. Street-level shops receive more maintenance because of the higher commercial rental income. People who once both lived and worked in the medieval part of the city now live elsewhere and commute to their jobs. This increases the congestion and air pollution. As the population has shifted from the city center to the suburbs, maintenance funds have likewise shifted. The more affluent areas of the city demand and receive a greater proportion of the resources available. In the meantime, homeless people have taken up residence in abandoned houses and apartment buildings as well as abandoned mosques. This is possible because of Cairo's mild climate and infrequent rain.

To reverse the trends mentioned above, it is necessary to not only preserve and retrofit the historic mosques but also rehabilitate the historic houses and apartment buildings in these districts. Although the mosques are the pivotal buildings in these historic districts, the vast majority of these districts consist of residential buildings. Without these buildings, the streetscape of the districts would be greatly diminished and the character and fabric of the districts would be irretrievably altered.

The leaking water- and sewer-pipes in Cairo and the resulting high ground-water table are well known. The water table is currently about one meter below the surface. Cairo has undertaken a massive project to install new sewers and water supply-lines throughout the city. Unfortunately, medieval Cairo was not one of the first areas of the city to receive these new services. Construction in these areas is only commencing now. I have been told that the good news is that the level of the ground-water table is going down in those areas of Cairo that have received new sewer and water services.

For some time, the ground water has been wicking up into the foundations and walls of these historic monuments. When these monuments were first built, the ground-water table was much lower. These buildings usually have substantial foundations. Excavation of the foundation of at least one building shows a course of impervious granite that would act as a moisture barrier. Unfortunately, the ground-water level is now above the level of the granite and migrating up through the porous limestone walls. This is known as "rising damp" and is one to two meters above the ground in most areas and higher in others. The soluble salts from the soil and the stone migrate to the surface as capillary action replaces moisture that evaporates at the surface. As the soluble salts evaporate, the salts recrystallize. Great quantities of salts can accumulate on the surface of the stone, called efflorescence. The crystals change from crystalline compounds to a powdery state through loss of water in crystallization when exposed to the air. Since the stone is very porous, the crystals can also form within the pores of the stone. Frequently, the salt crystals are larger than the pores. The formation of crystals behind the surface of the stone is called subflorescence, causing the surface of the stone to spall or flake off.

Pollutants are also deposited on the surface of stone from the air. Where the surface of the stone is totally dry, the stone is only discolored as the deposits increase. Where the surface of the stone is moist, the pollutants are converted to mild acids that eat away the surface of the stone by dissolving the binder in the stone causing the stone particles or grains to separate and erode away easily. Although there are other minor contributing causes of stone deterioration, such as bird droppings and impact from carts and automobiles, these appear to be negligible in the medieval area of Cairo. Moisture in the masonry walls also leaches the lime out of the mortar between the masonry units causing the mortar to crumble.

Frequently, people use water to try to wash the white efflorescence from the stone. This does not work. The water dissolves the salts and they soak into the stone and into the soil only to come to the surface of the stone again. Once the stone is dry, the white powder should be removed from the stone by dry brushing with a natural bristle brush, not allowing the powder to fall on the ground. Wire brushes should not be used because they abrade the surface of the stone and remaining fragments of the wire imbedded in the stone will rust and further discolor the stone. The powder that is brushed away should be collected in a dust pan or vacuum and removed from the site. A poultice may also be used to remove salts and stains from the stone. As the poultice slowly dries, the salts migrate to the surface. Once dry, the poultice will crack and fall off in some areas. It may be necessary to scrape off any poultice that remains on the surface of the stone. Whether the poultice falls off or is scraped off the stone, the dried poultice should be collected with a dust-pan or vacuum and removed from the site because it contains salts that can re-enter the stone if and when it becomes wet.

The high ground water has another potentially damaging effect. It is my understanding that the level of the water table (along with size and shape of soil particles and distribution of different particle sizes) is one of the factors that determine or contribute to liquefaction. The high ground-water level in the Cairo area seems to put the area at greater risk for liquefaction during an earthquake.

Restoring individual monuments without looking at the larger picture is not wise. The water problem in Cairo is not just a cosmetic problem. If the water problem is not solved and/or the seismic retrofit of the structure is not integrated into the restoration, much time, effort, and money may be wasted doing cosmetic work. The problems need to be studied and massive efforts initiated to provide permanent solutions. However, if we wait until the problems are solved, many monuments will undoubtedly be lost. Monuments on the verge of collapse cannot wait several years while major problems are studied and solutions initiated. Emergency stabilization and protection are treatments that will buy time to study the problems, arrest or lessen the causes of deterioration, and allow the environment to stabilize.

In their current condition, what are the monuments capable of withstanding? The more deteriorated a building is at the time of an earthquake, the less resistance it has to seismic loads, especially in the area of the deterioration. Localized failure may lead to progressive failure of part(s) or all of the structure.

To determine if the solutions to various problems are producing the desired results, the resources need to be systematically monitored and documented. For example, to determine if a water problem has been solved and the building is drying out, it is necessary to monitor the moisture content of the masonry by taking moisture readings at various locations at periodic intervals.

Systematic monitoring and documentation do not automatically imply high technology or low technology, but appropriate technology. For restoration, the use of new high-technology materials that have a very short track record may lead to far worse catastrophes in the near future when applied to monuments originally built of low-tech materials. Dekosit, a "miracle" product of the early 1970s, was used to patch the sandstone at Renwick Gallery in Washington, D.C., and soon the patches were popping off the building because the new product was physically incompatible with the original material.

The use of computer programs to compile and analyze voluminous quantities of data from monitoring and studying various problems may be very cost-effective. Equipment used to study, test, and monitor may vary from low-tech to high-tech depending on the situation and cost. If low-tech, inexpensive methods work, it is usually cost-effective to use them and save high-tech, more expensive methods for those situations where low-tech methods are ineffective or nonexistent.

Many of these Cairo resources have withstood one or more earthquakes. Just because a building has survived one earthquake does not mean it will survive another. The structure may have been damaged and weakened by the last earthquake. The next one may be more intense, last longer, have an epicenter that is closer, and/or have vibration waves that approach the structure from a different direction.

What are the inherent strengths and weaknesses of these resources? There are many factors that determine the extent of damage during an earthquake. One important factor is the shape and configuration of the building. For example, round and square buildings are usually equally strong to resist loads applied from any direction. This is one of the reasons that domes tend to respond well during an earthquake. Likewise, rectangular buildings that are almost square are stronger to resist loads applied to the building in the direction of the longer dimension. However, rectangular buildings that are much longer in one direction are much stronger to resist loads applied to the building in the direction of the longer dimension and much weaker to resist loads applied to the building in the direction of the shorter dimension. L-shaped, T-shaped, H-shaped, and E-shaped buildings have unequal resistance in different directions and usually have stress concentrations at re-entrant corners, the location of frequent damage during an earthquake. The more complicated and irregular the shape and configuration of a building, the more difficult it is to analyze and the more likely it will be damaged during an earthquake because of its uneven strength and stiffness in different directions.

There is usually more than one way to solve a problem. In order to preserve as much of the historic fabric and character of these resources, it is wise to develop various alternatives and evaluate them as to their effect upon the resource and their cost-effectiveness. What can be done with the least amount of money that will save lives and reduce future damage?

Wood-frame buildings usually respond well during an earthquake because they hold together and ride out the earthquake like a box. Wood in Egypt has always been very scarce and there are very few wood-frame buildings. Therefore, the problems of wood-frame buildings during an earthquake, such as shifting off their foundations, and their seismic retrofit, such as bolting the wood-frame superstructures to their foundations, will not be discussed.

Unreinforced masonry buildings, in general, react poorly in an earthquake and need to be tied together to help them retain their structural integrity. During an earthquake, masonry walls crack and sometimes crumble with dislodged bricks and stones falling from minarets, parapets, walls, and projecting balconies and ornaments, injuring or killing people and damaging other parts of the building and/or adjacent buildings. In addition, if the earthquake is strong enough or lasts long enough, the ends of wooden floor beams and roof rafters or trusses may shift out of their masonry pockets and collapse.

San Francisco, California, has had a parapet ordinance for over ten years. This ordinance required the owners of buildings to tie the parapets back to the roof. This has been found to be an extremely cost-effective method of preventing damage and loss of life. Almost all of the parapets that fell during the Loma Prieta earthquake in 1989 were from buildings outside the area of the city that required parapet-bracing. A masonry parapet is a vertical cantilever. A pishtaq on a mosque is a rectangular screen rising above a roof line and framing a portal or an iwan. A pishtaq is a perforated parapet. When unrestrained during an earthquake, the movement of the parapet may cause localized failure, which can eventually lead to catastrophic failure if the earthquake is strong enough or lasts for a long time. Bracing the parapet usually consists of tying the top of the parapet back to the roof by a diagonal steel angle. It must be noted, however, that this can only be done if the roof is in sound condition. Many of the roofs we observed after the Cairo earthquake of 12 October 1992, were in such deteriorated condition that the roof would have to be repaired or totally reconstructed before the diagonal bracing could be anchored to the roof. The advanced deterioration of the roofs is a very serious matter. The floors and roof of a typical building help brace the wall. These, of course, should be retrofitted with anchors to secure the floor system and roof system to the masonry walls so that the wooden members do not pull out of their masonry pocket during an earthquake. When the roof and upper floors of buildings are so deteriorated that they are about to collapse, they provide very little in the way of bracing to the masonry wall. Instead of having an unbraced parapet of one or more meters above the roof line, in reality there is an unbraced wall and parapet reaching vertically three or more meters.

If an earthquake is strong and/or lasts for a long time, not only may parapets fall but also the ends of wooden roof rafters and trusses and floor beams and girders may also pull out of their pockets in the masonry wall and collapse on the rooms and people below. When the masonry walls are not braced by the roof and floor structures, they are very tall vertical cantilevers, and progressive and catastrophic failure of the building can result. San Francisco, Los Angeles, and other cities are now requiring that floor and roof systems be bolted to the masonry walls. There are many different ways of doing this with exposed or hidden anchors.

Anchoring roof and floor systems to the masonry walls usually consists of drilling through the masonry wall and installing bolts that are fastened on the interior to the wooden members and on the outside with an anchor plate. The anchor bolts are usually grouted in place with a cement or epoxy grout. The drilled holes are usually not much larger than the diameter of the bolts and are horizontal to the earth.

Hidden anchors were originally developed for party walls on a property line, where access to the other side of the party wall is not possible. Instead of drilling a hole slightly larger than the anchor bolt, a hole three to four inches (8 to 10 cms.) or more in diameter is drilled two-thirds to three-quarters of the distance through the wall at a 22.5-degree angle (either up or down from the horizontal). A nut is placed on the end of the bolt and grouted in place, usually with cement. Tests on hidden anchors give results roughly equivalent to through bolts. The angle is for two reasons: it provides more resistance in pull-out tests and is easier to install. Since hidden anchors do not penetrate through the masonry and leave a hole on the other side, this method is frequently used for the faces of historic buildings where anchor plates would detract from the appearance of the buildings. This method of seismic retrofit is sometimes referred to as the bolts-only method, regardless of whether through bolts or hidden bolts are used. In rooms of a building where there is no finished ceiling, there may be easy access to install the bolts, and the bolts and their attachment to the floor and/or roof systems may be exposed with little adverse effect on the historic character of the room. In rooms of a building where there is a finished ceiling, either plain or ornate, it may be necessary to dismantle and install or recreate parts of the ceiling along the wall in order to drill the holes for the bolts. Care must be taken to minimize the loss of historic fabric.

The bolts-only method is not a "do it yourself" approach. Engineering calculations need to be done to determine the design loads, the size and spacing of the bolts, and the design of the detail connections. Bolts-only may be sufficient for small, regularly shaped (round, square, rectangular) buildings, but calculations are necessary to determine if this method is adequate. Larger buildings also require roof and floor diaphragms and shear walls or bracing. Diaphragms can be added on the top of the roof or floor or on the ceiling below (both provide equivalent strength for horizontal forces). If the ceiling below is significant, then the diaphragm may be installed on the floor above. If the flooring above is significant, it can be installed on the ceiling below. If both the flooring and the ceiling are significant, then a decision must be made as to which one can be disassembled and reconstructed with the least damage to historic materials.

The design, construction, and location of shear walls and bracing (X-bracing, K-bracing, etc.) must also be engineered taking into account the inherent earthquake-resistant characteristics of the building. Significant interior spaces should be avoided, if possible, when looking for locations to add shear walls and bracing. Care must be taken to avoid damage to significant historic fabric. Care must also be taken to ensure that certain parts of the building are not made significantly stiffer than other parts. If they are, there may be additional damage during an earthquake caused by the uneven stiffness. Sometimes these shear walls or bracing can be located in insignificant spaces. If not, other solutions or ways to mitigate the intrusion of the new structural members need to be developed.

Domes, vaulting, and minarets present special situations for retrofit that need special study and consideration. For some regular, free-standing buildings, base isolation can be used to reduce the effect of the earthquake forces on the building. This requires construction of a new foundation under a building resting on isolators that dampen the vibrations of an earthquake. It also requires the construction of a dry moat around the building so that the building can move slowly in any direction; therefore, only free-standing buildings can utilize this method.

We encourage the retrofit of historic buildings. Various approaches and methods have been used effectively to retrofit historic buildings. Just as there are no inappropriate materials, only inappropriate places or situations for almost any material, an effective method of retrofitting one historic building may not be appropriate for another. By developing and evaluating several (at least two) alternative retrofit solutions, one can determine which method is the least destructive to the historic character and fabric of a particular building. A thorough understanding of the resource and its significance is also very important.

What is it that we are trying to save? Identification of the most important spaces and features of a building helps the designer determine what to avoid and where retrofit elements may be added with the least effect on the resource. As stated before, this does not mean that all other spaces and features of historic building are fair game for demolition. We must also look at the cumulative effect of loss of historic materials even if these materials are replaced in kind. If the handle on our grandfather's ax has been replaced three times and the blade twice, do we still have our grandfather's ax? However, if I or anyone else replaced the handle and blade, then it is no longer my grandfather's ax. How much original historic material can be lost and still have a historic building?

What criteria or standards should be used to evaluate alternate proposed solutions? We will assume all proposed solutions provide an adequate level of life safety. If not, those that do not and cannot be modified for adequacy should be eliminated. Of those solutions that are adequate, we should choose the one that has the least adverse effect upon the character and fabric of the resource. In 1964 the Second International Congress of Architects and Technicians of Historic Monuments adopted what is commonly known as the *Venice Charter*. Neither the United States nor Egypt signed this document, but the *Venice Charter* is frequently recognized as the international standard for evaluating the preservation of historic monuments. The United States adopted its own standards: the Secretary of the Interior's *Standards for Preservation Projects*. It is my understanding that the Islamic nations met in Lahore, Pakistan, in 1980 and adopted the *Lahore Statement*. I do not know if Egypt adopted the *Lahore Statement*.

The Secretary's *Standards* provide definitions for the treatments of acquisition, protection, stabilization, preservation, rehabilitation, restoration, and reconstruction, as well as standards for each treatment. The *Standards for Rehabilitation* were revised slightly in 1990.

Acquisition is defined as the act or process of acquiring fee title or interest other than fee title of real property (including the acquisition of development rights or remainder interest). If the current owner of a property cannot or does not want to care for the resource or wants to demolish it, it may be necessary to acquire the property to save it.

Protection is defined as the act or process of applying measures designed to affect the physical condition of a property by defending or guarding it from deterioration, loss, or attack, or to cover or shield the property from danger or injury. In the case of buildings and structures, such treatment is generally of a temporary nature and anticipates future historic preservation treatment; in the case of archaeological sites, the protective measure may be temporary or permanent.

Stabilization is defined as the act or process of applying measures designed to reestablish a weather-resistant enclosure and the structural stability of an unsafe or deteriorated property while maintaining the essential form as it exists at present.

Preservation is defined as the act or process of applying measures to sustain the existing form, integrity, and material of a building or structure, and the existing form and vegetative cover of a site. It may include initial stabilization work, where necessary, as well as ongoing maintenance of the historic building materials.

Rehabilitation is defined as the act or process of returning a property to a state of utility through repair or alteration that makes possible an efficient contemporary use while preserving those portions or features of the property which are significant to its historical, architectural, and cultural values.

Restoration is defined as the act or process of accurately recovering the form and details of a property and its setting as it appeared at a particular period of time by means of the removal of later work or by replacement of missing earlier work.

Reconstruction is defined as the act or process of reproducing by new construction the exact form and detail of a vanished building, structure, or object, or a part thereof, as it appeared at a specific period of time.

Both the *Venice Charter* and the Secretary of the Interior's *Standards for Preservation Projects* require that the historic character and fabric of the resource be respected and preserved. There are some basic principles that underlie these criteria. These are the principles of minimal intervention, reversibility, compatibility, authenticity, and documentation.

The principle of minimal intervention states that we will never have any more historic fabric, with few exceptions, than we have today and that each time we do work on a building there is usually a net loss of historic fabric; therefore, the less we do to a building usually means the less the resource loses historic fabric. There are two exceptions. One is when original or early historic fabric, previously removed for whatever reason, is returned to its original location and reinstalled in an appropriate manner. The other is when new material added to a historic resource gains its own significance through time and events. This is more rare and usually takes a considerable passage of time.

To evaluate various proposals, we should try to assess which solution or solutions have the least adverse effect upon the historic character and fabric of the resource. Changes to a building can usually be categorized as additive or subtractive. When materials are added to a resource, the character and integrity of the resource may or may not be affected. When materials are removed from a resource, there is almost always a net loss of both historic fabric and integrity, and usually a loss of historic character also. If it is the removal of an inappropriate prior addition, it may be restorative in nature. Treatments that are additive in nature are usually more tolerable and acceptable, if reversible, because they can usually be removed at some future date. On the other hand, treatments that are subtractive in nature are usually not reversible, especially as the amount and significance of the materials removed increase. Heroic treatment should be reserved for those historic buildings that need massive intervention to save them. In Cairo there are some monuments that may be lost if heroic efforts are not made soon to protect and stabilize them.

The principle of reversibility states that nothing should be done to a resource that cannot be undone at a future date with little or no damage. We are usually not the first people to work on a historic resource and probably not the last. With the passage of time, we often learn how to do things better. Previous treatments to historic resources may now be causing more harm than good. To halt the damage or deterioration caused by a previous treatment, it may be necessary to do radical surgery, which may result in the loss of historic fabric. By designing treatments to a resource that are easily reversible with little or no damage, we are preventing or diminishing the future loss of historic fabric.

Anything that is done to a historic resource should be compatible or harmonious with the historic character and fabric. Compatibility of materials is very objective and based upon the matching of physical characteristics or properties, for example, weight, strength, coefficient of expansion and contraction, porosity, absorption rates, etc. The properties of the new materials need to be compatible with that of the historic materials so that the new materials do not damage the historic ones. Compatibility of historic character, on the other hand, is more subjective and based upon similarity of visual characteristics such as color, texture, size, scale, mass, proportion, configuration, rhythm, ratio of solids to voids, ornamentation, details, etc. If few or none of the characteristics of the new material harmonize with the historic materials, the effect may be very jarring and detract from the artistic and architectural expression of the historic resource. If all of the visual characteristics are matched, it becomes very difficult to distinguish what is historic and what is new.

Authenticity relates to integrity. Even a very fine replica can never be the "real thing." The original fabric of a resource is authentic and therefore has significance. It may be much less expensive to demolish the original resource and construct a replica with new materials and technology that looks just like the original resource, but a replica is always a replica. When the original material is lost, we lose the original craftsmanship and the patina of time. Replacements of missing parts of the design must be based on physical or photographic documentation, not conjecture. Even in a restoration, the replacement of missing parts must be compatible and an accurate replication but also distinguishable from the original so that the restoration does not falsify the artistic or historic evidence. This is frequently done by thorough documentation of the work and by labeling the new materials in an inconspicuous location, usually on the back.

Before we preserve anything, we need to know and understand the resource. Therefore, we must identify the resource and retain it. This also includes identification of the components of the resource that are the most important, such as significant spaces and features including skilled craftsmanship.

In reading the history of many of these monuments and especially the minarets, it is obvious that we are not the first people to work on these resources and undoubtedly not the last. It is extremely important that we pass these resources on to the next generation with as much integrity and in as good condition as possible. Likewise, it is extremely important that we document the information we have compiled, the problems we have studied, the alternatives we have developed and evaluated, the decisions we have made, and the results of our work (future monitoring), and pass this documentation on to future generations.

The purpose of this presentation was to look at the major problems facing Cairo's irreplaceable cultural monuments and to explore how to approach the solutions necessary to secure the future survival of these resources.

In the future, we will not be judged on how much we know, but on how we have used the knowledge we have to save these irreplaceable cultural resources. The work that we do to preserve and retrofit these resources will not only save lives but also allow us to pass our cultural heritage on to future generations.

Priorities in Selecting Restoration Sites: An Urban-Conscious Approach

Ahmed S. Ouf

Egypt's earthquake of 12 October 1992 was another warning to the Department of Antiquities that serious restoration measures are needed to safeguard the nation's heritage. Islamic monuments, specifically in Cairo, surfaced as a sector in need of extensive restoration work, since whole districts of the old city were affected. Entire streets are currently blocked with wood and metal bracing and struts to prevent buildings from collapsing until some idea of what should be done can be established. Most of Shari' al-Mu'izz between Bab al-Futuh and Shari' al-Azhar and most of Shari' al-Ghuriya, Shari' al-Mugharbilin, and Shari' al-Khayamiya ending with Bab Zuwayla show examples of the extensive damage that does not only need to be dealt with on a building-by-building basis but requires an urban-conscious perspective to restore the buildings and the urban tissue around them.

If a monument collapses, a piece of information may be erased from the nation's memory; but if the tissue of a whole street or district is altered, an entire historic era may drop from the nation's cognition of its heritage. The urban tissue of a city is an open book of the community behavior within its living quarters, the community's interaction with its subcultures through daily and periodical activities, the city's governmental systems, and the city's role within the nation. Consequently a decision about where to start restoration within the city is in fact more important a decision than how to restore a specific building.

The Current State of Islamic Monuments

It has only been since the late 1970s that sizable budgets have been deployed for restoration and upgrading of the overall national urban stock. Long years of war and limited national resources, coupled with a rapid rate of urbanization, have negatively impacted the maintenance and improvement of the existing urban stock during the last four decades. The "new cities" approach has also contributed to the general lack of interest in existing urban areas since most of the available budgets were directed to the new urban frontiers on desert land. Another urban concern during the last couple of decades was the dilapidated informal urban quarters to which most of the available funds from national and international organizations were channeled. Consequently, Islamic monuments did not receive the proper attention, as they are mostly located within the congested districts of the old city.

The 1990s should be the decade of the old city districts, not only for the provision of more liveable urban space but also for the preservation of the national heritage. Expenditures in this direction should be justified as a continuation of the large national cultural projects that were achieved during the 1990s such as the opera house, Nasr City conference complex, Cairo's Olympic village, and so on. It should also be seen as a priority expenditure since most of the existing Islamic monuments might not withstand another earthquake.

Results of the building surveys carried out by the staff of the Engineering Center for Archaeology and Environment (ECAE) and the staff of the Faculty of Engineering at Cairo University showed that most of the 150 Islamic monuments on the Department of Antiquities priority list are in need of immediate restoration to preserve them for another generation. Some of them such as the mosque of Ulmas al-Hajib (130), the house of 'Ali Katkhuda (540), the madrasa of al-Ghuri (189), the madrasa of Inal al-Yusufi (118), the mosque of Mahmud al-Kurdi (117), and Silahdar mosque (382) need now-or-never restoration efforts since they are subject to structural failure. Preliminary results of the emergency surveys performed by the ECAE staff immediately after the earthquake are summarized in table 1.

Recent surveys conducted by the staff of the Faculty of Engineering showed like results since most of the monuments had a similar crack and failure pattern, and architectural detail deterioration to those in the ECAE surveys. Table 2 shows a sample of preliminary survey results that were conducted by staff members of the Faculty of Engineering, Cairo University.

The information in the tables concerning the most recurrent cracks shows that stone arches had the highest percentage of crack occurrences among all surveyed buildings. Arches with metal or wood ties had less structural problems than arches that were not tied. Wall and component separation at corners was also obvious in most buildings showing that buildings were treated as "grouped three-dimensional components" more than holistic structures. Structural stability was derived from the harmony of the different building components and its heavy weight more than from the good connections among these components. Stone domes and vaults had the least cracks of all other components since they mostly carried only their own weight. Walls of the domed and vaulted chambers showed more cracks in the walls than separation at the corners, which makes us assume that their connections were better constructed than in other walls. From an architectural point of view, we might conclude that buildings with multiple arches that do not

Type of problem	34	190	381	117	129	540	218	118	224	130	239	382	189	43	187
Partial collapse				■	■	■		■		■	■	■	■		■
Wall cracks	■	■	■		■	■	■	■	■	■	■	■	■		■
Wall separation	■		■	■		■	■	■		■	■	■	■		
Floor settlement		■		■		■	■	■			■	■	■		
Wall dampness		■	■		■			■		■	■			■	■
roof dampness		■	■		■	■	■		■				■	■	■
Arch key crack	■	■	■			■	■		■	■	■	■	■	■	■
Arch separation	■	■	■		■	■				■	■	■	■	■	■
Improper restor	■		■		■		■			■	■		■		
Dome crack											■				
Vault crack	■								■						
Minaret collapse						■								■	
Minaret tilting							■					■			

Table 1. Sample of the Surveyed Monuments, by the ECAE Staff, Cairo University.

Type of problem	109	358	65	66	67	410	190	332	192	359	72	185	203	368	191
Partial collapse	■	■			■									■	
Wall cracks	■	■	■	■			■	■	■	■			■	■	
Wall separation	■								■		■				■
Floor settlement		■			■	■						■	■		
Wall dampness	■		■	■					■			■	■	■	
roof dampness									■			■	■		
Arch key crack	■		■	■	■		■	■			■	■		■	■
Arch separation	■														
Improper restor		■	■				■	■	■			■	■		
Dome crack									■						■
Vault crack															
Minaret collapse															
Minaret tilting															

Table 2. Sample of the Surveyed Monuments, by the Staff of the Faculty of Engineering, Cairo University.

support a dome or a vault should receive higher priority in restoration than those which do. Buildings that originally had domes that are now lacking—such as the madrasa of Sultan al-Ghuri—become more susceptible to earthquake damage than domed buildings because the very three-dimensional components that form the overall structure are weakened.

Architectural Priorities for Restoration

From an architectural point of view, a monument does not need to be structurally collapsing to be in need of quick intervention. A monument that starts losing its authentic flooring material (al-Kurdi mosque, Baybars al-Khayat mosque, al-Ghuri kuttab and sabil, etc.), its authentic roofing material (Gunbulat mosque, Silahdar mosque, Sarghatmish mosque, etc.) or even the authentic wall texture by covering it with a thin layer of plaster (Baybars al-Khayat mosque, al-Kurdi mosque, etc.) is actually loosing the very characteristic that gave it historic value in the first place. For example, Baybars al-Khayat mosque does not have serious structural problems outside the mausoleum dome; however the whole building needs re-restoration to remove the recent cement plaster work and bring it back to its original stone look. Mahmud al-Kurdi mosque is another example of a building that is structurally sound but almost completely modernized by the use of new building materials in its floor, walls, and roof.

Architectural and decorative details of Islamic monuments are the very essence of their beauty and the conveyors of the symbolic and cultural messages embodied in each building. They tell us about the craftsmanship, technology, and cultural symbolism of their era. "Fine restoration" of details is normally more expensive and more time-consuming than any structural restoration that a building might need. The loss of a detail while doing structural restoration of a building might be irreversible since it is practically impossible to recreate such details with modern technology and craftsmanship. If anything should happen to alter the original marble patterns of the mausoleum of al-Ghuri, mosque of Gunbulat, or the Qalawun complex, it would be very expensive—if the proper craftsman were to be found—to recreate them. It might take an entire lifetime to bring a single building to its original architectural condition even if the money were available. A surviving monument after good structural restoration but with lost details on the ceiling, floor, and walls is a worthless, empty shell. Consequently, the preservation and restoration of fine architectural details should be viewed as a priority of structural restoration because they keep the monument culturally significant. Buildings with endangered architectural and decorative details (e.g., muqarnasat, wall and ceiling calligraphy, window and door carving, etc.) should be given high priority in restoration.

Historic value of each monument is another determining factor in prioritizing any building for restoration. Buildings that are one of a kind, such as the maq'ad of Mamay (51), palace of Amir Bashtak (34), hammam of

Sultan al-Mu'ayyad (410), and Musafirkanah (20) should have high priority since they represent building types that might be lost of they collapse. Priority should also be established to cover buildings from different historic periods: early Muslim, Fatimid, Bahri Mamluk, Burgi Mamluk, Ottoman, and Khedival. Fatimid mosques have already received intensive restoration efforts during the last decade through funds provided by the Bohari group. The very few monuments surviving from the Fatimid period or earlier should receive top priority because most of the Islamic monuments in Cairo belong to Mamluk periods or later. Since most Mamluk monuments are in similarly bad structural condition, the architectural value and the urban location of the buildings must become strong factors in determining their worthiness for restoration, rather than simply their structural condition. Buildings from the Khedival period are more abundant, structurally sound on average, and should receive lower priority for restoration.

Community Participation

A very important issue that restoration consultants should keep in mind while preparing their vision of the required restoration schemes is that most—if not all—Islamic monuments are still being utilized by local communities. Unlike pharaonic monuments, which might be closed off until restoration work is completed, Islamic monuments continue to function as prayer halls during restoration work. Parts of the mosques that were braced off after the earthquake to secure their structural shbility are still operating for daily prayers, such as in the mosque of al-Sanbugha, and Zawiyat Najm al-Din and Inal al-Yusufi mosques. Local communities have always been willing to maintain Islamic monuments because of their functional utility, as can be seen clearly in the new cement-tiled flooring and cement plaster of Fayruz mosque, al-Kurdi mosque, Inal al-Yusufi mosque, etc. The needs of the local communities put pressure on the Department of Antiquities to intervene within a reasonable period of time. If a building is left in a state of bad disrepair too long, the local community may step in and get the job done in a less than satisfactory way through its own limited financial and technical resources.

It has been noticed during the monument surveys that improper restoration was apparent in many buildings because of the local unwillingness to see the buildings deteriorate while they wait for the proper official restoration work to take place. Most common improper restoration work was the utilization of modern building materials (e.g., cement plaster, red brick, floor-tiles of cement and crushed marble, concrete roof slabs, etc.) and the addition of whole new building components (e.g., new washrooms, ablution fountains, rooms for mosque imams and servants, etc.). Community participation needs to be directed and encouraged; it is a good sign of cultural continuity and an underestimated source of funds.

Prioritizing, scheduling, and delegating restoration tasks might be important in this respect as they allow community funds to be directed to specific and measurable tasks within a well-defined framework of restoration activities. Sinan Pasha mosque in Bulaq, al-Sanbugha mosque, and Zawiyat Najm al-Din are some examples of monuments for which local communities expressed explicitly a strong desire to take over the responsibility of all restoration work once the Department of Antiquities approves a work plan. Consequently, community participation should be encouraged and considered a priority factor as it guarantees good maintenance of the monument · after restoration. Local funds should be utilized in visible restoration to establish a communal sense of achievement and responsibility for the monument.

Urban Priorities in Cairo

In a complex city like Cairo it is very difficult—if not impossible—to have a comprehensive plan within which all restoration work might be implemented. A dynamic structure plan is the most that a practical planner might think of achieving to guide restoration efforts that cannot wait for a comprehensive vision to be prepared. Metropolitan Cairo already has a structure plan in which the city is seen as a metropolis of many homogenous sectors. Massive efforts that are currently underway to improve Cairo's urban condition such as the subway lines, the sewage tunnel, and the ring road are all funded by international organizations according to a priority list prepared by the General Organization for Physical Planning (GOPP). Being concerned with the restoration of Islamic monuments on that metropolitan scale means directing funds to the upgrading and improvement of the homogenous urban sector that contains the old city districts. Some major urban projects within that sector are already passing the document production phase and are ready for implementation, such as the al-Azhar restoration project, Aga Khan Islamic Garden in the al-Darrasa hills, north al-Gamaliyya development project (Bab al-Nasr cemetery), and the al-Mu'izz Street development project. Unlike projects on the metropolis scale, such sector projects are not implemented within a general view of their environmental impact on each other. These projects are not prioritized according to an old city urban structure plan but rather chosen by the various funding agencies since capital is considered the scarcest of all resources. Being practical means that an incremental and accumulative planning approach within an urban structure plan is called for to prioritize future urban restoration and conservation projects. In order to set up criteria for prioritizing restoration work on the structure plan level of the historic city, an urban-conscious approach needs to be adopted to determine for each monument the following issues: its urban impact on other ongoing upgrading efforts; the possibility of creating new tourism routes; the impact of restoration efforts on the local communities; the possibility of soliciting funds from different funding agencies for the same urban-focused restoration and upgrading efforts; and the expected cost-recovery cycle.

My proposal here is for either a "location-bound" selection in which the concerned agency—let it be the Organization for Upgrading the Fatimid and Islamic Districts of Cairo, together with the Department of Antiquities—selects a quarter of the old city to take priority over other quarters in monument restoration. Or it may choose a "linear" approach in which a street or an urban corridor gets priority in restoration for all its monuments, street layout, and community buildings. Both strategies are capable of producing a practical and feasible structure plan for the historic city area. They also direct restoration efforts to reduce any disadvantages that might arise from disjointed incremental efforts and allow good possibilities for collaboration between all concerned agencies (see table 3). Applying either of these two urban-conscious strategies, in addition to the basic structural/architectural priority listing, should be enough to guide restoration work and improve old Cairo's structure.

Islamic monument restoration in Egypt is an issue that will face generations to come since the magniitude of the problem is much greater than the resources available to a single generation. An accumulative incremental approach that does not wait for a comprehensive plan to be prepared before restoration work begins is often the only approach possible.

The role of the Department of Antiquities in directing restoration efforts should start by preparing a priority list for all buildings that determines the urgency of all structural, architectural, and fine restoration that each building needs. The surveys of 150 monuments that were recently conducted by the

LINEAR	LOCATION-BOUND
- Upgrade important buildings on a specific street segment	- Upgrade all buildings within a specific locality
-Community improvement limited to connections between monuments	- Community improvement is extended to the whole urban area
- Local activities would not be incorporated unless opening directly on the specified "line"	- Local activities are incorporated within the overall restoration scheme
- More appropriate to funding by agencies concerned with Islamic monuments alone	- Opens up funding possibilities for local improvement works by different funding agencies
- Increases short-term pay backs from tourism with feasible fiscal commitments	- Reduces short-term pay backs from tourism and requires large sums of initial cost
- Money recovery cycle is short but community benefits are limited	- Money recovery cycle is long but community benefits are far-reaching
- Politically significant since results are short-term	- Politically unsafe since results are long-term
- Requires less community participation and can easily be managed by the existing concerned agencies	- Requires extensive community creation work and needs large scale management efforts by different concerned agencies

Table 3. Linear and Location-Bound Restoration Approaches Compared

staff of the Faculty of Engineering might work as a good base for this priority list, if augmented with the proper architectural and historical points of view. A rough cost-estimate might also be important since it will help the funding agencies and the local communities determine their capabilities in financing specific restoration tsks for a single building or group of buildings.

My proposed priorities are as follows:
— endangered structures that might not withstand another earthquake
— buildings with weakened three-dimensional structural components
  through the loss of a dome, a vault, or a cracked retaining wall
— buildings with endangered architectural and decorative details
— buildings that represent a building type, for example, wikala,
  hammam, etc.
— buildings from periods earlier than the Mamluk era
— Mamluk or later buildings whose locations impact the overall urban
  fabric of the city according to a linear or a location-bound scheme
— buildings for which local funds might be solicited as the community
  indicates an intention to maintain the building long-term.

The proposed urban-conscious approach for prioritizing monument restoration efforts, whether location-bound or linear, allows for directing the monument restoration efforts to work as city-wide upgrading efforts. It is not the scope of this paper to evaluate both scenarios and decide which might be better in tackling the problems of Islamic monument restoration in Cairo. However, I recommend a pilot project on a stretch of al-Mu'izz Street between Bab Zuwayla and the mosque of Ganibay to evaluate the linear scenario. This project would contain monuments numbered 190, 395, 199, 203, 116, 406, 407, 117, 557, 118, 314, and 119. A location-bound strategy might be attempted on the whole area behind al-Azhar mosque containing monuments 75, 76, 74, 103, 77, 96, 445, 73, 71, 466, 69, 64, 63, 98, and 351. Both areas would open new tourism routes within the historic city and would extend considerably the time spent by tourists in the area, which is generally limited now to a visit to al-Azhar mosque and the Khan al-Khalili area. In-depth study of the possibilities of adding both areas to the tourism route within Cairo, initial cost, and the impact of their restoration on local development would be necessary to finalize the decision on which approach to take.

Resources

Survey documents published by ECAE, Cairo University for the Egyptian
   Antiquities Organization, December 1992 and January 1993.
Survey documents and photographs by the Faculty of Engineering, Cairo
   University, for the Egyptian Antiquities Organization, 1993.

The Impact of Environmental Pollution on the Mosque of al-Azhar and the Complex of al-Ghuri

Abd El-Zaher A. Abo El-Ela

Orignially the Islamic monuments of Cairo were built on stable soil and in favorable environmental conditions.[1] As population increased, so did the number of buildings, and a variety of new, unfavorable changes began to afflict these historic buildings.[2] For example, the nature of the soil under foundations changed. The soil became saturated with waste and sewage water and the subsoil water caused deleterious changes in soil properties, which ultimately undermined the stability of buildings. This created vertical and oblique micro- and macro-cracks in main walls and contributed to severe structural failure in Islamic monuments.[3] The aim of this study is to consider all the factors that have played a dominant role in the deterioration of the mosque of al-Azhar (A.D. 972), built by Gawhar, a general under the Fatimid Caliph al-Mu'izz li-Din Allah.[4] This study also will discuss the impact of the deterioration on the al-Ghuri complex (A.D. 1503), located at al-Azhar and al-Mu'izz streets.[5] This complex consists of the madrasa–mosque, called "the hanging mosque." It contains a cruciform plan and four liwans, of which the qibla iwan is the largest. Sections of the mausoleum dome, kuttab, sabil, maq'ad, houses, and wikala have been destroyed.

Topography of Cairo

Cairo consists of low-lying areas frequently inundated by sewage water, which has serious adverse affects on Islamic monuments.[6] The soil on which the foundations are built is mixed with rubble. Moreover, these sites have been flooded by water from lakes and canals, such as the Egyptian canal (now Port Said Street). These canals were connected to wells. All of them have now been demolished but they became a source of subsoil water, which penetrates to the lower parts of foundations and walls of Islamic monuments.

Hills are located to the east of Cairo at 55.5 meters above sea level. Salah Salem Street is 50 meters above sea level and at its lower sections along al-Azhar Street at a level of 49 meters, and at al-Gamaliyya Street at a level of 30 meters to 15 meters sloping to the west. The ground water in this area is relatively deep (about 21 meters). The water table in the last ten years has risen about 1.50 meters to a depth of 19.50 meters. The underground Metro project, constructed between 1982 and 1985, affected the level of the water table, which was lowered because of pumping operations.

Due to the unplanned expansion of Cairo and the increase in water use (about four million cubic meters of water), while the capacity of sewage lines remains at about two million cubic meters, there is much more waste water. Saline water and organic matter have been added to the subsoil water causing damage and loss of soil components, seriously affecting the monuments in Cairo. All of these objectives indicate that sewage water is the principal reason for the severe deterioration of the soil and consequent destruction of Islamic monuments.

Factors Causing Deterioration

Foundation Weakness
Foundations consisting of heterogeneous materials create a relatively unstable soil. This, unfortunately, is the type of soil under most of the Islamic monuments.[8] It contributes to the formation of vertical and oblique micro- and macro-cracks in walls and other architectural elements. Moreover, serious leaning of some minarets is also present.

Sewage Water and Salts
In fact, sewage water contains different destructive salts (chlorides, sulfates, nitrates), which cause the deterioration of the building materials used in Islamic monuments.[9] These soluble salts migrate through the materials of buildings from the soil by the capillary system to a considerable height in the walls of historic buildings. Because of evaporation, soluble salts deposit on or beneath the surfaces of stones and crystallize in different phases, causing various types of deterioration.[10]

Air Pollution
Air pollution plays a major role in the deterioration of building materials used in historic buildings.[11] For instance, Cairo is surrounded by various industrial sites. Thirty kilometers to the south of Cairo is Helwan, where different factories produce iron, steel, coke, chemicals, automobiles, and cement.[12] To the north of Cairo are Shubra al-Khayma, Musturud, Abu Zabal, and an electrical power station. In this area factories produce dyes, textiles, glass, ceramics, and metallic and chemical products. All of these factories emit different pollutants (gaseous, liquid, solid), which are carried by the dominant winds (north and northeast, and west or south, southwest) down to Cairo, where many of the historic buildings are located.[13]

Concentration of Particles and Gases

The heavy industry of Helwan produces different kinds of pollutants.[14] The dust particles on the ground surface at Helwan were 478 tons/mile/month in 1988. This was 24 times more than the world system (15 tons/mile/month). Its aerosols were 1988 million particles/air m^3, which was 30 times more than the world system (60 million particles/air m^3). Carbon dioxide (CO_2), is about 0.04 ppm, and the concentration of ozone (O_3) is 124 micrograms/air m^3. Cement industries produce severe pollutants such as calcium dust, sulfates, chlorine, and free silica dust.

At Shubra al-Khayma, Musturud, Abu Zabal, and at the electrical power station different kinds of pollutants are produced.[15] Dust particles on the ground surface are 150 tons/miles/month in 1988—10 times more than the world system—and this is made worse by the high concentration of the heavy elements, cadmium, lead (70 ppm of lead dry weight). Sulphur dioxide (SO_2) is more than the world system 10 pp/100 m. All of these pollutants, carried by dominant winds down to Cairo, quicken the rate at which building materials used in Islamic monuments deteriorate.

Every day Cairo receives a high dose of pollutants composed of 52 percent monocarbon oxide (CO), 14 percent sulphur dioxide (SO_2), 21 percent hydrocarbons, 10 percent dust, solid material, and 2 percent (NO_x) nitrogen oxide.[16] Heavy traffic was about 300,000 cars in 1984 and the dust particles from the Muqattam hills to the east of Cairo was 27 gr/m^2/month in 1962. This increased to more than 60 gr/m^2/month in 1988, with a particularly high amount in the summer when the aerosols of dust in the air were more than 500 micro-gr/m^2/month.[17]

Reactivity of Gases

Carbon dioxide (CO_2) in rain water dissolves the calcium and magnesium carbonates in limestone, dolomite marble, lime mortars, and plasters[18]

$$CaCO_3 + CO_2 . H_2O \rightleftharpoons CO (HCO_3)_2$$

$$MgCO_3 + CO_2 . H_2O \rightleftharpoons Mg (HCO_3)_2$$
(insoluble)   (soluble)

Nitric oxide (NO_x) is the most abundant and stable atmospheric gas, but it enters into chemical reactions under special conditions such as high temperature or pressure. Nitrous oxide (N_2O) is produced in soils and water by microbiological processes, where free nitric acids interact. The carbonate rocks are converted into calcium nitrate according to the following chemical reaction:

$$CaCO_3 + 2HNO_3 \rightleftharpoons Ca (NO_3)_2 + H_2O + CO_2$$

Sulphur oxides (SO_x) can be represented according to the following:

$$S + O_2 \rightleftharpoons SO_2$$

$$2SO_2 + O_2 \rightleftharpoons 2SO_3$$

Normally, water vapor is present in sufficient amounts to combine with SO_3 to form droplets of sulfuric acid:

$$SO_3 + H_2O \longrightarrow H_2SO_4$$

Gaseous sulphur dioxide is absorbed by calcareous stone and oxidized on its surface.[19] The stone surface would rapidly saturate with sulphur dioxide at normal atmospheric humidity. The erosion process associated with calcium sulfate formation would be virtually continuous and form gypsum.

$$SO_3 + CaCO_3 + 2H_2O \xrightarrow{\text{catalyst}} CaSO_4 . 2H_2O + CO_2$$

Deterioration at the Mosque of al-Azhar

Soil under the foundation of the mosque of al-Azhar was saturated by sewage water, which carried different kinds of salts. The unstable leaning of some columns, cracks in some arches, and the collapse of some of the Fatimid stucco ornaments have been caused by the penetration of ground moisture in the walls and to the disintegration of some marble pedestals around the open court, which are subjected to sun rays (figs. 1, 2).[20]

Some samples have been collected and investigated by x-ray diffraction. The results reveal the presence of different compounds: calcite, gypsum, sodium nitrate, sulfate, sodium chloride, and traces of quartz (fig. 3). All of these compounds indicate the combination of sewage water and air pollutants, which leads to the formation of new phases of minerals and causes severe deterioration of building materials.

Deterioration of the al-Ghuri Complex

The madrasa–mosque has been severely affected by sewage water and abuse by human activity. It was seriously damaged in the earthquake of 12 October 1992.[21] The main reason for such damage is the high groundwater table. The saline water has a deleterious effect on the foundation of the mosque of al-Ghuri, leading to uneven settlement of the foundation and structure, as well as to the heterogeneous component of the soil under the foundation (depth of 3.4 meters). In addition, there are vertical and oblique cracks, especially in the basement floor where there are shops and liwans of the madrasa–mosque. Moreover, some walls and the minarets are leaning.[22] Various kinds of salts, moving through the foundations by capillary action at a high level in the walls, cause severe deterioration such as powdering of the stone blocks, fallen marble dados, and biochemical damage to the wooden ceiling (figs. 4, 5, 6, 7).

The collected samples from the madrasa–mosque have been investigated by x-ray diffraction, which shows the presence of $NaCL$, NaN_{03}, $CaSO_4$, $CaSO_4.2H_2O$, and FeO, KNO_3 (fig. 8) and some other crystalline salts from the mausoleum dome and wikala (figs. 9, 10). All of these deposited salts show the relation between ground water and air pollution.

Notes

1. S. Beilke, and G. Gravenhorst, "Cycles of Pollutants in the Atmosphere," Symposium Physico-Chemical Behavior of Atmospheric Pollutants, Ispra, 16–18 October 1979.
2. H. Azzah, "Environmental Pollution Produced from Industrial Areas, Greater Cairo City," Second Symposium on Environmental Study, Ain Shams University, 1990 (in Arabic).
3. "Cracking in Buildings," *Building Research Establishment Digest* 75 (1976).
4. K.A.C. Creswell, *The Muslim Architecture of Egypt*, vol. 1 (London, 1951).
5. A. Hassan, *History of Archaeological Mosques* (1946) (in Arabic).
6. H. Kamal, "Ground Water Attacks Islamic Monuments," *al-Alam al-Gadid* "Development and Environment," 48 (1990) (in Arabic).
7. "Damp-Proof Courses," *Building Research Establishment Digest*, 77 (1971).
8. A. Ezzat, "Towards Global Treatment of the Islamic Monuments in Cairo," *Symp. Arab. Cont.* (1993) (in Arabic).
9. A. S. Saleh, "The Effect of Subsoil Water on the Deterioration of the Stone of the Sphinx, Aeroport," paper presented to the Egyptian Organization of Antiquities, Jan.
10. "Rising Damp in Walls: Diagnosis and Treatment," *Building Research Establishment Digest* (1986); E. M.Winkler, *Stone: Properties, Durability in Man's Environment*, second edition (Vienna, 1975); G. Torraca, "Porous Building Materials," *Material Science for Architectural Conservation*, second edition (ICCROM) (1982).
11. Abd El-Zaher A. Abo El-Ela, "Conservation of Stones and Stone Buildings on the Giza Plateau with Reference to the Sphinx and One of the Site Tombs," (Ph.D. dissertation, Cairo University, 1989) (in Arabic).
12. M. Ahmed, "Effect of Pollution by Cement Products on Metal Scales," *Second Symposium on Environmental Study* (Ain Shams University, 1990) (in Arabic).
13. "The Assessment of Wind Speed Over Topography," *Building Research Establishment Digest* (1984).
14. International Center for Research, paper on environmental pollution in Helwan (1988) (in Arabic).

15. Raafat, I., "Facing Problems in Shubra al-Khayma, Replanning 1966," (Cairo University: Planning Faculty, 1989) (in Arabic).
16. E. Alaa, "Environmental Protection in Egypt," *Development and Environment* 24 (Sept. 1989) (in Arabic).
17. F. Hassan, "Environment in Egypt," *Development and Environment* 26 (Nov. 1988) (in Arabic).
18. G. G. Amoroso, and V. Fassina, "Stone Decay and Conservation, Atmospheric Pollution, Cleaning, Consolidation and Protection," *Materials Science Monographs* 11 (1983).
19. D. J. Spedding, "Sulphur Dioxide Uptake by Limestone," *Atmos. Environ.* 3 (1969).
20. A. Arnold, "Behavior of Some Soluble Salts in Stone Deterioration," second international, Athens, Gre(ece, 1976; "Cracking in Buildings," *Building Research Establishment Digest* (1976); Creswell, *The Muslim Architecture of Egypt*; "Damp-Proof Courses," *Building Research Establishment Digest* (1971).
21. Hassan, *History of Archaeological Mosques*.
22. Ezzat, "Towards Global Treatment of Islamic Monuments in Cairo."

Fig. 1. Crystalline salts, carried in ground water that wicks up into marble pedestals, cause the stone to deteriorate in the al-Ghuri complex.

Fig. 2. Destruction to entrance caused by crystalline salts from ground
water in the al-Ghuri complex.

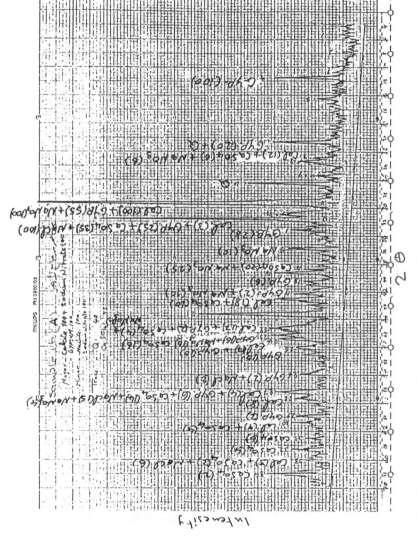

Fig. 3. Sample of x-ray diffraction pattern for al-Azhar mosque.

Fig. 4. Cracking of lower lintels in the mosque of al-Ghuri.

Fig. 5. Disintegration of limestone caused by salt deposits from ground water in the al-Ghuri complex.

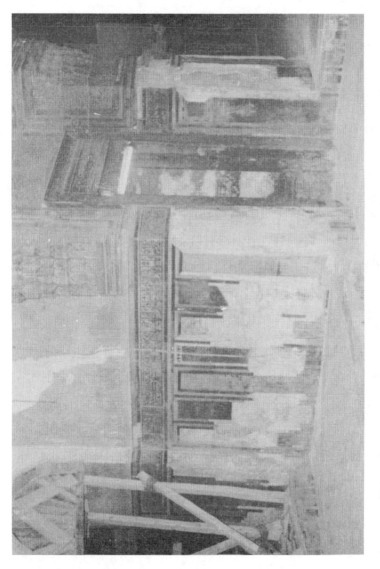

Fig. 6. Collapse of marble dados caused by salt deposits from ground water in the al-Ghuri complex.

Fig. 7. Deterioration of supporting member (wikala) caused by salt deposits from ground water in the al-Ghuri complex.

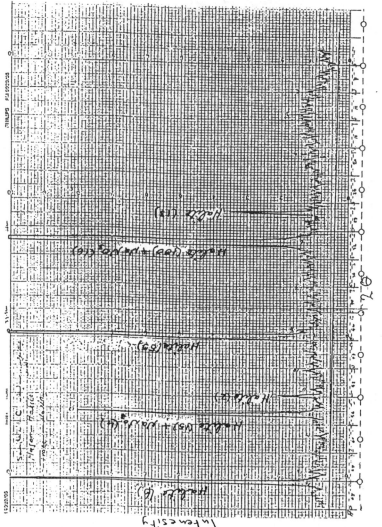

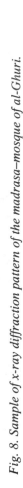

Fig. 8. Sample of x-ray diffraction pattern of the madrasa–mosque of al-Ghuri.

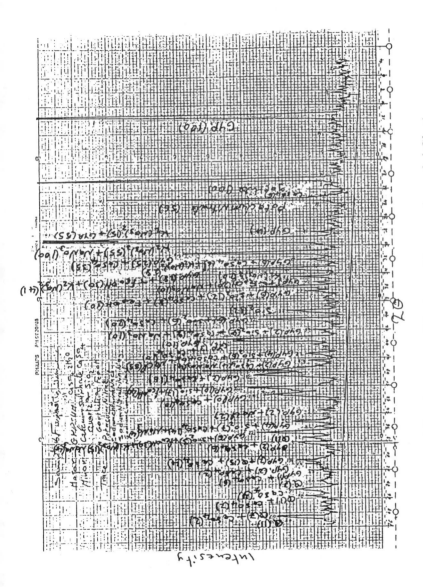

Fig. 9. Sample of x-ray diffraction pattern of the dome of the mausoleum of al-Ghuri.

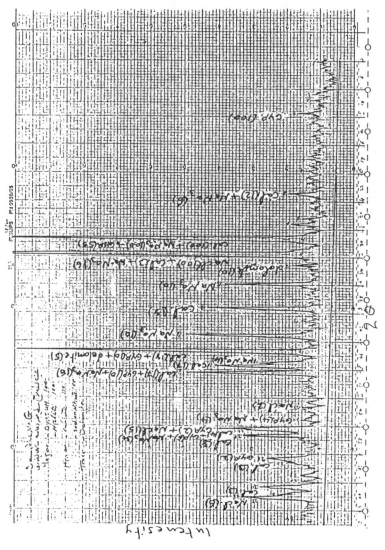

Fig. 10. Sample of x-ray diffraction pattern of a supporting member (wikala) in the al-Ghuri complex.

Ground Water and the Deterioration of Islamic Buildings in Egypt

Mohammed Abd El-Hady

This paper studies the serious role of ground water in the deterioration of historic buildings in Egypt as well as the sources of this water and the formation of crystalline salts in the building materials. This study will be helpful in selecting and developing suitable conservation techniques for prolonging the lifespan of historic buildings.

Ground water, subsoil water, or subsurface water are general technical terms referring to the water or moisture that attacks historic buildings from the soil on which they are built. Ground water in lesser or greater quantities is present everywhere in the soil, subsoil, and the bedrock. It is either of external origin (derived from atmospheric or surface waters) or internal origin (derived from the interior of the earth). The greatest amount of ground water comes from atmospheric precipitation and is called meteoric water. The water retained in sedimentary rocks from the time when they were originally laid down is termed connate water. Water liberated as a result of igneous activity, for example during the crystallization of magma, is called juvenile water.

The amount of ground water entering the ground varies greatly from place to place and is determined by the following factors: (1) amount and nature of the rainfall; (2) slope of the land surface; (3) porosity and permeability of the surface layers; (4) rate of evaporation; (5) amount of vegetative cover; and (6) amount of water already in the soil.

Deterioration of Building Materials Caused by Ground Water

Ground water and the soluble salts are considered the most damaging factors in stone decay. The very complex capillary system of stone and the often strange paths of moisture in the different building materials complicate the understanding of the mechanism of deterioration, such as salt migration, salt crystallization, salt hydration, and so forth. In the absence of water, there would be (1) no chemical reaction of stone constituents; (2) no soluble salts would be transported or would migrate, crystallize or recrystallize; and (3) no air pollutants would dissolve in the droplets and change into acidic solutions, which cause serious damage to the carbonate stones. In fact, there is a direct correlation between the movement of water within the pores of stone (capillary rise) and the porosity of the stone, where the porous stones commonly absorb large amounts of water—more than semi- or non-porous stones. On the other hand, the amount of water that penetrates into stones, its transport, as well as its exchange rate with the atmosphere, depend on, among other factors, the geometry of the stone's pore system.[1]

The continuous variations of air temperature and relative humidity of the surroundings have a systematic effect on the suction mechanism in stones. With increasing evaporation rates in the surroundings caused by hot climatic conditions, the capillary head drops, whereas conditions that inhibit evaporation will shift it upward.[2] It is known that the building stones in monuments are porous materials and characterized by a wide range of porosity ranging between 50 percent and a few percent. The porosity of stone causes permeability to water and water vapor: the degree depends on the capillary structure of the stone.

Transport of Ground Water in Porous Stones

The movement of water in a porous body is proportional to the volume of empty spaces. In reality, the movement of water through the pores of stones depends on the capillary system. It also is known that the suction pressure increases as the diameter of the pores decreases and is very large for pores with a diameter less than one micrometer. This phenomenon is called capillary suction. The cause of the capillary suction is the attraction of water toward the walls of the pores. The reason for the attraction of water molecules to the walls of pores is that most porous material contains oxygen atoms, which carry negative electrical charges or hydroxyl groups that are polar because the oxygen atoms are more electronegative than the hydrogen atom. Pore surfaces with polar atoms (oxygen) or groups of hydroxyl show strong electrostatic attraction for polar molecules, such as water surfaces that attract water molecules, which are called hydrophilic surfaces.

The strong electrostatic attraction created by the hydrogen atom is called a hydrogen bond. The attractive forces between the two charges is higher at points of contact between water molecules and hydrophilic surfaces. It is believed that frequently the surface oxygen is bound on one side to a hydrogen atom forming an 0-H group, which is called a hydrogen bond. This group carries both negative (on oxygen) and positive (on hydrogen) electric charges.

Water molecules attracted to the surface by an oxygen atom would turn their positive side toward the surface itself. In the case of surface hydroxyl groups, attraction of water molecules both to the positive hydrogen and the negative oxygen is possible. But the attachment from the positive side of the water molecules should prevail even in this case because the oxygen can form two hydrogen bonds while the hydrogen can form only one.

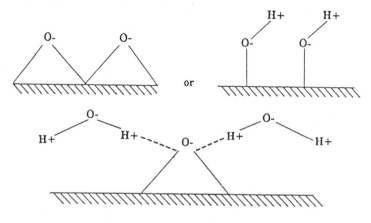

Hydrophilic Surface

Ground water penetrates inorganic building materials at varying degrees. Over time it destroys them through the mechanism of rhythmic transport of soluble salts to the surface of building stones. Their subsequent dissolution is caused by the condensation on that surface from humid air or by rainfall.[3]

The rise of moisture by capillarity exposes masonry walls to the deterioration and to salt impregnation. The maximum height of capillary rise is often marked by a white efflorescent ring or dark wet margin, which remains wet as the salt concentration at this level tends to hold the moisture for a long time.

Natural stones may contain water-soluble salts entrapped in their pores as natural impurities. Salts can act in stone in several different ways, influenced by the mode of its travel, temperature, and concentration. Ionic diffusion of salts can take place as diffusion in water-saturated stone from areas of higher ionic concentration toward areas of lower concentration. In fact, it is believed that there is a connection between soluble salts and the chemical decay phenomena. Their quantity and quality seem to be indicative of current processes of physiochemical attack. According to Arnold and Zehnder, the salt solution in walls is complex. Its concentration and composition vary greatly.[4]

The local ionic compositions, mainly Na, K, Ca, Mg, CO_3, SO_4, NO_3, C_1, etc., determine the normally crystallizing salt species that are precipitated according to their solubility in the area where salt solution evaporates. Due to the evaporation of salt solutions, the crystalline salts are deposited whenever their water solution becomes oversaturated. The crystalline deposits are precipitated in the available space of a given pore and if water evaporation continues, all dissolved salts are precipitated.[5]

Efflorescence on Stone Surfaces

Blotches, patches, and margins of white salts on the walls of buildings form unpleasant-looking layers. Soluble salts crystallize at the surface at the open ends of capillary systems. Generally, saline crusts are deposited on most surfaces of building stones used in historic buildings in Cairo. Such crusts are less than one millimeter thick, but in certain cases their thickness may grow to several millimeters or even to a centimeter.

Chemical analyses carried out on the limestone samples collected from many historic buildings in Egypt showed that chlorides and the sulfates of calcium and magnesium are the most common salts among water soluble salts in stone. The crystallization of soluble salts on the surface of stone is due to the low rate of ventilation or the high air temperature in the surroundings, which cause the evaporation of saline solutions. In this case the salt crystals are formed mainly outside the pores of stone.

The conditions that govern the position of crystallization depend to some extent on the nature of the salts, on the texture of the building material, and on the conditions of evaporation. The salts are deposited internally if the surface evaporation takes place over a relatively short time. The terms cryptoflorescence or subflorescence are used to describe the crystallization of soluble salts within the pores of stone.

Soluble salts are very mobile, moving along the surfaces of historic buildings as well as in and out of stone surfaces. These movements occur periodically according to the season and the amount of precipitation and absorption of water. The most intense deterioration caused by salts occurs when wet to dry cycling is most frequent. The expansion of the crystalline salts induced by the mechanism of hydration is met with resistance from the pore walls of stones. This opposite pressure influences the salts by obstructing the enlargement of volume.

The hydration pressure of salt is very harmful to building materials. When the relative humidity increases in the surroundings, hydration takes place. The absorption of water increases the volume of salts and thus develops pressure against the pore walls. Thus the hydration pressure depends on temperature and humidity changes in the surroundings. For example, the co-aversion of anhydrous calcium sulfate brings about a 32 percent increase in volume, which this may lead to the corrugation and crumbling of the building materials.[6] Ground water becomes a very destructive element, which causes serious damage to historic buildings when other physicochemical factors of deterioration such as air pollution and micro-organisms are present.

The Effects of Ground Water and Air Pollution

The physicochemical deterioration caused by air pollution to building materials is controlled by the occurrences taking place at the interface of sulfuric or sulfureous acid/solid material. A direct result of this contact is the conversion of calcareous stones to gypsum.

Ground water is considered one of the catalysts that is responsible for creating the wet phase in which the various gaseous pollutants can convert into acids. For example, carbon dioxide in the air or that produced by industrial activities can dissolve in water and change into carbonic acid. This weak acid is responsible for dissolving calcium or magnesium carbonate when it attacks limestone, marble or dolomite and forms calcium and magnesium bicarbonate according to the following equation:

$$CaCO_3 + CO_2.H_2O \rightleftharpoons Ca(HCO_3)2$$

$$MgCO_3 + CO_2.H_2O \rightleftharpoons Mg(HCO_3)2$$

Nitrogen oxides play a dominant role in the deterioration of the carbonaceous materials. These acids can convert into nitric or nitrous acid in the presence of moisture. According to B. S. Lal, in the regions where free nitric acid occurs, its prolonged action will affect building materials by converting carbonates into nitrates.[7] For example, calcium carbonate can convert into calcium nitrate when attacked by nitric acid.

Sulfur dioxide is considered a very common gaseous pollutant in the atmosphere of industrial regions. In the presence of moisture, sulphur dioxide is hydrolyzed and changes to sulfuric acid, which is able to change calcium carbonate into calcium sulfate when it attacks carbonaceous materials.

The Effects of Ground Water and Micro-Organisms

Biodeterioration is a very common phenomenon on the wet surfaces of building stones attacked by ground water. Bacteria, fungi, and lichen spores are abundant on these stones. It is obvious that ground water, after penetrating historic buildings in Cairo, creates ideal conditions for the growth of micro-organisms, which likewise absorb large amounts of water. Water accounts for about 70 percent of the weight of these micro-organisms. Moreover, micro-organisms produce different kinds of organic acids such as carbonic, oxalic, sulphuric, and nitric acids, which play a dominant role in destroying the mineral constituents of the building materials.

It can be concluded that ground water is considered one of the main sources of moisture present in building stones and that it plays a dominant role in carrying soluble salts from the soil to these stones. In addition, ground water is considered the catalyst for the crystallization of soluble salts and the growth of micro-organisms on the surface of stone and the conversion of air pollutants into serious acids, which cause severe damage to the building materials.

Notes

1. J. Ordaz, and M. R. Esbert, "Porosity and Capillarity in Some Sandstone and Dolomite Monumental Stone," *Fifth International Congress on Deterioration and Conservation of Stone* (Lausanne, 1985), pp. 93–100.
2. D. Hoffmann, and K. Niesel, "Moisture Movement in Brick," *Fifth International Congress on Deterioration and Conservation of Stone* (Lausanne, 1985), pp.103–10.
3. R. J. Schaffer, "The Weathering, Preservation, and Restoration of Stone Buildings," *Journal of Royal Society of Arts* 111 (1955), 843–67.
4. A. Arnold, and K. Zebnder, "Crystallization and Halite of Salts Efflorescence on Wallsu," *Fifth International Congress on Deterioration and Conservation of Stone* (Lausanne, 1985), pp. 269–77.
5. T. Stambolov, "Effect on Sulphur Pollution on Building Materials," *Conference on Museum Climatology* (London, 1967), pp. 15–21.
6. H. Mortensen, "Die saltz prengung und ihre Bedeutung", *Geog., Anstalt. Hrsg.* 79 (1933), 130–35.
7. B.S. Lal, "Weathering and Preservation of Ancient Building Materials," *Studies in Museology*, 12 (1979), 28–43.

Fig. 1. Damage caused by ground water and efflorescence to the porous limestone of the mausoleum of Qalawun.

Fig. 2. Ground water at the mausoleum of Qalawun wicks up the limestone walls, depositing thick saline layers which mix with particulates from air pollution.

Fig. 3. Contour scaling of the limestone in the madrasa of al-Ghuri, al-Azhar mosque, is caused by moisture from wicking ground water and crystalline salt deposits.

Fig. 4. Limestone blocks are rapidly deteriorating but marble blocks remain stable at the madrasa of al-Ghuri , al-Azhar mosque.

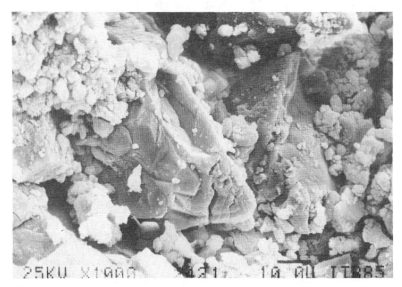

Fig. 5. Limestone samples taken from the mosque of al-Ghuri reveal under SEM micrograph the severe effects of ground moisture.

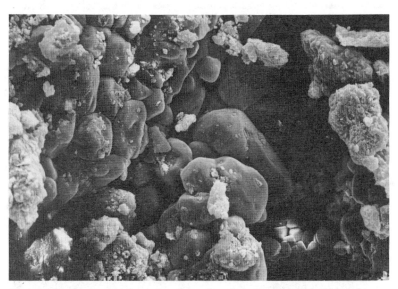

Fig. 6. Limestone samples taken from the mosque of al-Ghuri reveal under SEM micrograph the destruction caused by crystalline salts.

Structural Aspects of Damage to Islamic Monuments

A. A. Abdel Gawad
M. S. Hilal
M. Abou Kefa

The unusual earthquake of 12 October 1992 has triggered intense investigation into the safety of the Islamic monuments of Egypt, an invaluable national treasure long neglected. Fortunately, in most of the monuments examined, earthquake destruction was minimal. Nevertheless, extensive damage already existed at a number of sites (probably because we simply have so many of them). This paper briefly classifies the typical types of damage encountered according to their severity. It describes suggested approaches to overcome the geo-technical difficulties (high water table and soil weakness). It also presents a proposed methodology to analyze the structural types of damage.

Assessment of Types of Damage

The types of damage and/or failure revealed during the investigation could be classified according to their seriousness as follows.

Inconsequential Damage

Damage or problems of this type are of no immediate structural concern but they do need attention for the structure to maintain its durability. Examples of such damage are:

— Decomposition of the lime mortar between stone courses, and between adjacent stone blocks in walls. This is probably due to loss of adhesion of the mortar to the adjoining stone over time, combined with some slight relative motion.

— Partial wear of blocks made of friable or weak sandstone, mostly due to weathering.

— Dessication of new replacement stone blocks because of their poor quality and high porosity (fig. 1).

— Deterioration of stone and masonry blocks because of probable chemical aggression of gypsum plastering and/or air pollution (fig. 2).
— Old sporadic vertical fissures in thick stone walls.
— Slight old separation at intersections of walls.

Repairable Damage
In this category are damage or problems that need prompt action to avoid potential failure under any future overload or soil subsidence. Examples include:
— Disintegration of the lime mortar between stone blocks of arches and domes (fig. 3).
— Through cracks in stone blocks of lintels (fig. 4).
— Continuous vertical separation between stone blocks.
— Active settlement cracks at wall corners (fig. 5).
— Local failures in slender elements such as minaret marble columns (fig. 6).
— Disintegration of stones at wall intersections.

Overall Repair and/or Replacement
In this category are structures or parts of structures that have already collapsed, or where overall failure is imminent, such as:
— Severe thrust of domes or arches on abutments or walls.
— Excessive settlement that has distorted the structure (fig. 7).
— Tilting and/or displacement of wall corners due to excessive settlement (fig. 8).
— Disappearance of wooden floors or wall parts in areas where collapse has already taken place (figs. 9, 10).

Geo-Technical Aspects and Suggested Solutions
Most of the significant damage is caused by the high level of the ground-water table, which may cause either disintegration of foundations, walls, and columns on first floors. Moreover, excessive settlement may take place causing severe stress to these elements of the structure.

It is necessary to propose a method to control and to lower the surface-water level under and nearby existing buildings. The effects of lowering the surface water should be carefully examined. It is well known that installation of some spaced drains (horizontal drains) has a great effect on controlling the irrigation water level. The required depth of soil aeration for plant growth may he fully controlled by proper spacing of these drains. The same idea may be applied to control the fluctuation of the water table near important buildings. By proper spacing of horizontal drains, a dynamic equilibrium of the water table will be produced below a specified water table depth. Water will be drained by gravitational force without the need of any electrical or mechanical equipment.

Although the lowering and controlling of the surface water level will save foundations from deterioration, it may have a harmful effect on the building itself and the nearby buildings. This is caused by differential settlement, which often follows this kind of operation. Therefore, it is very important to monitor the building and adjacent buildings for a long period of time. Settlement points will be fixed on the structural elements for this purpose. Piezometers are also needed to monitor the ground-water levels.

Structural Aspects and Methods of Analysis

Evaluating the above-mentioned failures one can conclude that a detailed analysis of the structures needs to be carried out. This analysis may include the overall analysis of the structure or the analysis of its individual elements such as walls, arches vaults and/or foundations. The vertical loads including mainly the weight of the elements as well as the superimposed loads should be taken into consideration. The lateral load due to wind or earthquake is also included in order to evaluate how such structures sustain these loads. The effect of settlement and/or differential settlement on the structure and its surroundings due to the vertical movement of the ground water is also included.

It is clear that beside the overall analysis of the structure or its elements, a technique for local failures and the redistribution of the stresses should be adopted. Updating the redistribution of the local stresses and following up the failures step by step requires special techniques. One of these techniques is the finite element method, which will be summarized in the following sections.

The Finite Element Method

A structure or part of it (fig. 11) is divided into finite elements connected to each other at their corners (or nodes). The stiffness matrix [K] for such an element relates the nodal forces {F} to the nodal displacement {S}, i.e.:

$$\{F\} = [K] \{S\}$$

This equation represents the relation between the displacement {S} of the nodes of the element and the forces in that element {F}. The individual stiffness coefficients within [K] depend on the geometry of the element shape, area, and thickness, as well as the material properties—Young's Modulus and Poisson's Ratio. The member stiffness matrices [k], can be assembled into a structure stiffness matrix [K] using again the Direct Stiffness Method.

The vast majority of stress analysis problems can be categorized as (1) planar (plane stress, plane strain, axisymmetric solid); (2) three-dimensional solid; (3) plate bending; (4) shells; and (5) linkage element.

Planar

A planar problem is one in which the degrees of freedom are in the one plane only. This of course does not rule out the possibility of stresses in the third direction. Figure 12 shows a bulkhead in a boxgirder bridge for which the stresses due to inplane forces are needed. A combination of triangular and quadrilateral plane stress elements could be used in the idealization of this structure.

Only rarely does the engineer need to analyze a general three-dimensional solid. This is fortuitous because such an analysis can be expensive both in the computer costs and in the preparation of data. Figure 13 shows a single buttress in a dam that could be treated as a three-dimensional solid. Tetrahedral, or hexahedral, elements having three translational degrees of freedom at the corner nodes could be used for the analysis. It is worth noting that the high cost of three-dimensional solid analysis can frequently be avoided by the use of a simplifying assumption that reduces the problem to two dimensions.

Plate Bending
Flat slabs (fig. 14) are the most common examples of plate bending action. The finite elements used for the analysis of plates subject to normal loading have normal translation and rotations as degree of freedom. These elements evaluate the bending moments and shear forces in a slab.

Shells
A variety of finite element approaches can be used for the analysis of shells. The cylindrical roof of figure 15 can be analyzed by three different finite elements: (1) flat (facet) plate elements that combine plate bending and stretching behavior; (2) curved elements; (3) solid elements—these elements may have curved faces as shown. The relevant degrees of freedom are shown in each case.

Linkage Element
In the finite element analysis, the contact surface between two materials usually has common nodes that have the same displacements. This means that at the common nodes, there is no license for the relative movement that they hold by virtue of their interface shearing behavior. In order to overcome this shortcoming in the analysis, a finite element that can handle the interface behavior between two surfaces at the contact planes and allow for the independent displacement of the two materials is needed. The method of stiffness is basically the simple concept of using "bar" elements across the interface in both the normal and tangential directions. The following assumptions are made in the interface analysis.
— The element representing the interface between the two materials is of zero thickness.
— The element offers high resistance to compression with negligible deformation.
— The shear strength of the element comes from the friction between the two surfaces.
— The behavior of the element in shear defines the relative displacement of the two materials.

The linkage element shown in figure 16 has the four nodes: i, j, k, and l. Infinitesimal thickness and shear stiffnesses should be obtained experimentally. It is always possible to combine different element types together in the one idealization.

In particular, the stiffness method of analysis has demonstrated that the sequence of operations involved in using the method to solve a problem are independent of the type of the element being used. This point is very important since it means that computer programs may be written that are capable of analyzing a variety of problems provided. Of course, that assumes the correct types of elements are available.

Fig. 1. Interior wall, Jamin al-Bahlawan mosque, Shari' al-Surujiya. Inferior quality and high porosity of replacement stones are causing rapid deterioration.

Fig. 2. Qawsun gate, Shari' al-Surujiya. Stone and masonry failure
probably caused by gypsum plastering and/or air pollution.

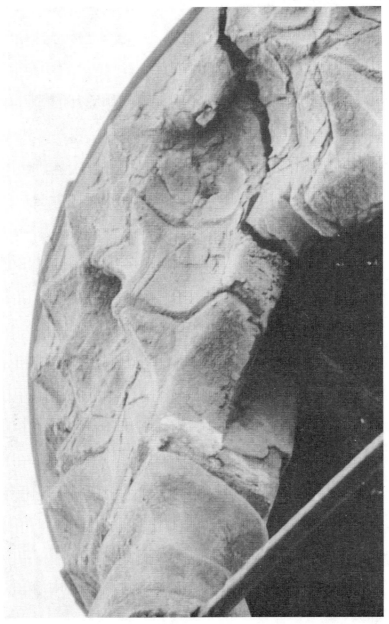

Fig. 3. Minaret, al-Kurdi mosque, Shari' al-Mugharbilin. Disintegrating lime mortar between stone blocks.

Fig. 4. Arch springing, al-Mas al-Hajib mosque. Through cracks in stone blocks and arches.

Fig. 5. Wall at corner of al-Sarghatmash mosque. Active settlement cracks.

Fig. 6. Sarghatmash mosque. Local failure in slender elements such as minaret marble columns.

Fig. 7. Arches of sahn, Sultan Shah mosque, Shari' Ghayt al-Idda.
Excessive settlement has distorted the structure.

Fig. 8. Corner of exterior wall looking from outside, Sultan Shah mosque.
Tilting and/or displacement of wall corners caused by excessive
settlement.

Fig. 9. House of 'Ali Katkhuda, Shari' Port Sa'id. Wooden floors and parts of walls have disappeared almost entirely where collapse has already occurred.

Fig. 10. House of 'Ali Katkhuda. Collapsed wooden floors and walls.

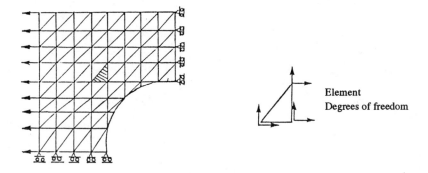

Fig. 11. Plate-stretching problem and finite element model.

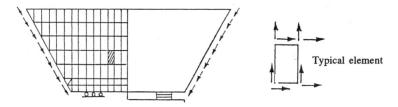

Fig. 12. Box girder bulkhead: plane-stress idealization.

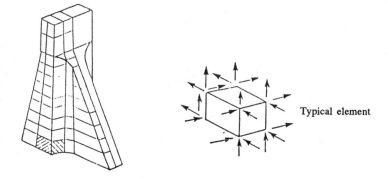

Fig 13. Dam buttress: three-dimensional idealization.

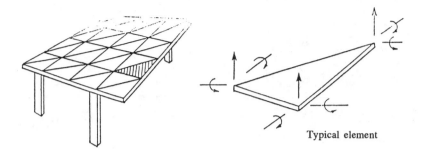

Typical element

Fig. 14. Flat slab: plane-bending idealization.

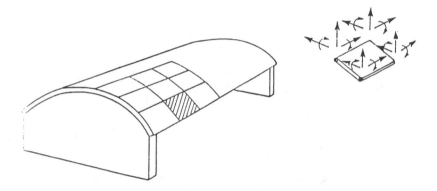

Fig. 15. Cylindrical shell roof: curved-shell idealization.

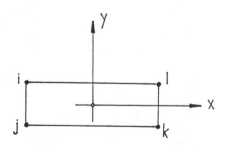

Fig. 16. Four-noded linkage element.

Restoration of the Mosque of al-Zahir Baybars in Cairo

Saleh Lamei

In the middle of al-Zahir Square stands one of the major congregational mosques in Cairo, built in the Bahri era by the sultan al-Malik al-Zahir Rukn al-Din Abu-l-Fath Baybars al-Salihi al-Najm al-Bunduqdari, born A.D. 1223/ A.H. 620 in Qipchak. He reigned from A.D. 23 October 1260/A.H. 16 Dhu-l-Qaʻda 658 until his death on A.D. 1 July 1277/A.H. 28 Muharram 676.[1]

The Site of the Mosque

The site of the mosque was selected by the sultan himself in the area known at that time as Qarqaus, located in the Husayniya district. He chose a suitable place for the mosque on his polo field. The Arab historian al-Maqrizi[2] tells us that after the Mongol invasion of Mesopotamia, many inhabitants of the region fled to Egypt, the majority of which were concentrated in the Husayniya area so that by A.D. 1296/A.H. 695 the district had become quite overpopulated.[3]

Baybars visited the site on A.D. 6 January 1267/A.H. 8 Rabiʻ II, 665 and plans were submitted to him for his approval. He ordered that the entrance should be similar to his school's entrance in al-Nahhasin and the wooden dome *(maqsura)* in front of the mihrab should be similar to that of the mausoleum of Imam al-Shafiʻi.[4]

According to our study, the maqsura was not only similar in shape to the mausoleum of al-Shafiʻi, but also in size and construction:

	Baybars	Imam al-Shafiʻi
Interior plan	15.4 x 15.4 m.	15.25 x 15.25 m.
Height of lower part	16.80 m.	16.35 m.
Wall thickness	2.70 m.	2.75 m.

According to the inscription on the marble slab in the tympanum, above the three entrance doors, the construction of the mosque was ordered on A.D.

12 June 1267/A.H. 14 Rabi' II 665, six days later than the date given by al-Maqrizi.[5] The construction began on A.D. 13 March 1267/A.H. 15 Jumada II 665, two months later than the date of the construction order.[6] The inauguration was in A.D. June 1269/A.H. Shawwal 667, so the entire construction of the mosque took twenty-seven months. Wood and marble were pulled from the ruined cathedral of Jaffa and were used in the construction of the dome and the encrustation of the mihrab.

Structure and Architecture of the Mosque

The mosque covers an area of about 10,000 square meters enclosed by a limestone wall about 10 meters high and 1.65 meters thick above the sill. A cornice of .35 meters terminated the façade, which was crowned by stepped crenellations atop a roof balustrade .87 meters high and .58 meters thick. The exterior curtain walls were built on the outer side by fine dressed stone and on the inner side by half-dressed stone *(talatat/batih)* and plastered. The filling consists of rubble stone with a clay-lime mortar.

In plan the mosque is of the Egyptian riwaq-type with an inner open large court *(sahn)*. There are six arcades on the qibla side, running parallel to the qibla wall, three are perpendicular to the qibla wall on the southwestern and northeastern side and only two are parallel to the qibla wall on the northwestern side.

The space in front of the mihrab is divided into two major compartments: the first was covered by a wooden dome, carried on piers with engaged columns at each corner, while the second compartment was arranged as a triple transept leading from the large inner court to the dome. The transept has a higher roof than that of the riwaqs and is similar to the transept roof, which leads from the main entrance in the northwestern façade to the inner court.

The mosque has three gates: the northeastern and the southwestern gates are smaller than the main one in the northwestern façade. Also, the roof of the transept of the secondary gates was a little bit higher than the riwaq's roof. Drawings done by Creswell show the mihrab angle at 143 degrees, whereas the qibla direction from Cairo is 135 degrees from the north.[8]

The mosque is simple and sincere in architectural expression. Monumentality and dignity are exhibited in the architectural treatment of the gates, while beauty and richness pervade its interior stucco ornamented friezes and its floral and geometrical gypsum lattice windows.

Only the skeleton of the original mosque remains in its walls, entrances, and the piers that once supported the wooden dome in front of the mihrab compartment. The rest of the mosque was rebuilt during this century.[9]

History of the Mosque

According to the historian Ibn Iyas (d. A.D. 1524/A.H. 930), the mosque was still intact during the sixteenth century.[10] Al-Jabarti (d. A.D. 1829/A.H. 1241) mentioned that in the seventeenth century Sufi meetings were held in the mosque.[11] During the French occupation, the mosque was used as a barracks and was known as the al-Zahir Citadel.[12]

At the beginning of the nineteenth century, columns and stones were stripped from the mosque and used in the building of the riwaq al-Sharaqwa at al-Azhar mosque.[13] In 1816, Muhammad Ali used the area as a soap factory and as a bakery. Later most of the buildings inside the mosque were demolished.[14]

According to the reports of the Comité de conservation des monuments de l'art arabe, interest in conserving and preserving the building began in 1892. But in 1901, the building was still being used as a slaughterhouse by the English army.[15] In 1908, the Comité began to document the architecture of the building.[16] In the same year, the Egyptian University asked the Comité for permission to build some classrooms for its students on the site. Finally in 1911, the English army vacated the building.[17] In 1915, plans were draw up to turn the area into a garden and these plans were implemented around 1920.[18] It was obvious by 1936 that the walls of the mosque had been seriously affected by the irrigation water used in the garden and they had badly deteriorated.[19] In the same year, an ambulatory was built inside the mosque.[20]

In 1940, members of parliament pushed for reconstruction of the mosque with preservation of its original form—especially the minaret—as its main goal. The project was voted down, however.[21] After 1956, the government built shelters for inhabitants of the area on the site.

Plans Preliminary to Restoration

Much preliminary planning and study has been done before any restoration of the mosque could commence. To begin with, thorough studies of of the mosque's history, structural elements, building materials, soil composition, and causes of deterioration were undertaken. These included:

History of the Mosque and Site
— Collecting data exhibited by the monument itself (traces of missing parts).
— Collecting data derived from the structure (wall thickness, foundation).
— Deducing data from the monument through the study of graphic surveys (e.g., French expedition drawings).
— Collecting data from published literature.
— Collecting data from graphical retrospective documentation (e.g., old photographs).
— Collecting data from documents and ancient manuscripts (Archive of the Comité).

Study of Soil, Structure, and Building Materials
Investigations of the soil and foundations were undertaken to determine the structural problems. The foundation is made of rubble stone with clay-lime

mortar. The depth of the foundation is 2.80 meters below the riwaq floor level.

Static analysis was done to study the stability of the building. The study of the static behavior of the building showed that a part of the southeastern wall above the sill has to be dismantled, as the inclination is more than 1 centimeter per meter height and exceeds 4 centimeters in the total height above the sill.[22]

A study of ground water in the area and its chemical analysis was done. Water samples taken from 3.00 depth were:

	Unit per million
Sodium chloride	497,000
Sulphur trioxide	610,000
HP	736

Physical and mechanical tests were carried out, as were chemical and mineral analysis of stone and mortar. Plaster tests were done for different samples of old mortar at the laboratory of the EAO. Test results showed that it consisted of one part slaked lime plus three parts sand. In some places it consisted of one part slaked lime plus two parts sand. We found that straw was mixed with the original plaster coat. All the new plaster work executed recently (1960–70) was done with cement mortar.

Mortar samples were taken from different areas—lower, middle, and upper parts of the building—from a wall depth of fifteen to twenty centimeters to get samples with constant humidity. The analysis was conducted by the EAO laboratory.

Stone test: conducted in the laboratory of the Department of Chemistry, Ministry of Industry
Density: 2.0 T/m^3
Porosity: 22.6 percent
Compression dry: 231 kg/cm^2
Sodium chloride: 0.1 percent
Abrasion test: for new flooring tiles according to Egyptian specification no. 269: 1.2 mm.

Tests showed that the density is low (good stone 2.6–2.7 T/m^3) and effective porosity in limestone varies 5 to 15 percent; therefore, the delivered stone samples were rejected.

Tests for wood in the reconstruction of the dome were done. It was mentioned in the tender that the company had to deliver pitch pine wood. A test on wood samples was done at Cairo University by the Faculty of Engineering. The delivered wood was not pitch pine and the ultimate stresses given by the laboratory were much less than the permissible stresses given by German specification, Din 1052 for wood class II. Therefore, the wood was rejected.

Wood	Permissible Stress, Class II	Ultimate Stress in Delivered Sample
Bending	100 kgcm	79 kgcm
Tension across grains	85 kg/cm^2	75 kg/cm^2
Compression along grains	85 kg/cm^2	60 kg/cm^2

Site and Building Survey
Site and building surveys were undertaken which determined different levels of the site and building as well as sewage and water supply lines; produced a complete set of drawings, plans, elevation sections, and details; reconstructed the missing parts and elements in accordance with the recommendations of the *Venice Charter* (1964).

The Permanent Committee for Islamic Monuments approved in its 19 December 1988 meeting the reconstruction of the wooden dome and the minaret, according to the study and drawings presented by our center.

Causes of Deterioration
Our research and study discovered and explored the reasons for the deterioration of the mosque and the site. Research showed the following.
— Fill soil was affected by surface water causing deformation in the soil and therefore unequal settlement in the bearing structure.
— Disintegration of masonry was due to salt corrosion as a result of rising humidity.
— Decomposition of the building binding mortar was due to rising dampness caused by capillary action.
— Reconstructed R.C. foundation and ties, done in the 1960s, were severely damaged by sewage water; reinforcement had completely rusted through in certain areas.
— The use of Portland cement, which contains calcium and aluminum silicates as well as calcium sulfate and some alkaline salts, had penetrated into porous materials causing damage, such as dark spots, efflorescence, and salts crystallization stresses.
— Repointing with Portland cement mortar had created a bond that was stronger than the building material.
— Deterioration of the roof coverings was due to humidity caused by rain.
— Deterioration of roof timber construction was due to biological and microbiological actions.

Restoration and Reconstruction Plan

Recognizing the problems inherent in the structural system of the mosque, the following consolidation and repair works were proposed.

Phase One
Consolidation of the foundation of the columns in the northeastern and southwestern sectors. Permissible stress on the soil at the foundation level for the reconstruction was 0.5 kg/cm².

Phase Two
Executing a de-watering project to decrease the surface water level from -0.20 to -1.00 m. below the original flooring level of the inner court in order to reduce dampness caused by capillary action.

Phase Three
Reconstruct a new concrete foundation for the missing northwestern and northeastern parts of the mosque
— Reconstruct R.C. columns in northwestern part covered by marble-stucco plaster. Marble columns are very expensive (L.E. 25,000 each).
— Reconstruct the original roof shape of the riwaq transepts as well as the wooden dome in front of the mihrab and all necessary architectural features.
— Reconstruct the minaret appropriate to the building, according to historical and architectural studies, taking into consideration the geometric analysis for examples built before and after this mosque during the Bahri era.
— Duplicate old mortar joints and repoint missing ones, retaining original masonry and mortar,
— Reproduce all exterior finishes and interior features that duplicate the original as closely as possible in size, color, and texture.

Notes

1. Abu-l-Fida' Isma'il, *al-Bidaya wa-l-nihaya fi-l-tarikh*, vol. 13 (Cairo, 1932), p. 222; al-Maqrizi, *al-Khitat*, part 2 (Bulaq A.H. 1270), pp. 229–302; Ibn Taghri Birdi, *al-Manhal al-Safi wa-l-mustawfi ba'd al-wafi*, vol. 3, edited by Nabil 'Abd al-Aziz (Cairo: General Book Organization, 1986), pp. 447–67, no. 717; Ibn Taghri Birdi, *al-Nujum al-zahira*, vol. 7 (Dar al-Kutub, 1938), p. 196; 'Abd al-Aziz al-Khurwaytir, *al-Malik al-Zahir Baybars* (Riyad, 1976); *Encyclopaedia of Islam (EI2)* (Leiden, 1960), vol. 1, pp. 1124–26; G. Wiet, *Biographies du Manhal Safi*, no. 708 (Cairo, 1932), pp. 102–3; S. F. Sadeque, *Baybars I of Egypt* (Decca, 1956); P. Thorau, *Sultan Baybars I von Aegypten* (Wiesbaden, 1987).
2. J. Bloom, "The Mosque of Baybars al-Bunduqdari in Cairo," *Annales islamologique* 8 (1982).
3. Al-Maqrizi, *al-Khitat*, part 2 (Bulaq, A.H. 1270), pp. 20–22.

4. Ibid., 299–300.

5. Combe, Sauvaget, Wiet, *Répertoire Chronologique d'épigraphie arabe* (Cairo, 1943).

6. Creswell, *Brief Chronology* (Cairo, 1919), pp. 79–80.

7. Van Berchem, C. I. A., MMAF 19 3/1 (Cairo, 1894), 121–22.

8. Bloom, "The Mosque of Baybars al-Bunduqdari," pp. 47–48, note 7.

9. Creswell, *The Muslim Architecture of Egypt*, (Oxford, 1959), p. 160.

10. Ibn Iyas, *Bada'i' al-zuhur*, 4 (Cairo, 1960), p. 161.

11. Al-Jabarti, *'Aga'ib al-athar* 1 (Bulaq A.H. 1297), p. 337.

12. Ibid., 3 (Bulaq A.H. 1297), pp. 33–34.

13. Ibid., 4 (Bulaq A.H. 1297), p. 162.

14. Ibid., p. 256.

15. Procès-verbal, Notebook 18, report 111 (1901), p. 126.

16. Ibid., Notebook 25, report 160 (1908), p. 46.

17. Ibid., Notebook 28, report 180 (1911), pp. 3–4.

18. Ibid., Notebook 32, report 539 (1915), p. 630.

19. Ibid., Notebook 38, report 717 (1940), p. 10.

20. The ambulatory was demolished in 1986 during the execution of the dewatering project.

21. Procès-verbal: Notebook 38, report 766 (1936–40), pp. 307–45.

22. The southeastern wall (height 10.70 m.) is inclined 0.35 cm.; therefore it was statically unstable.

Fig. 1. Southern entrance of the mosque of al-Zahir Baybars (1915).
Courtesy of the Visual Collections, Fine Arts Library, Harvard
University.

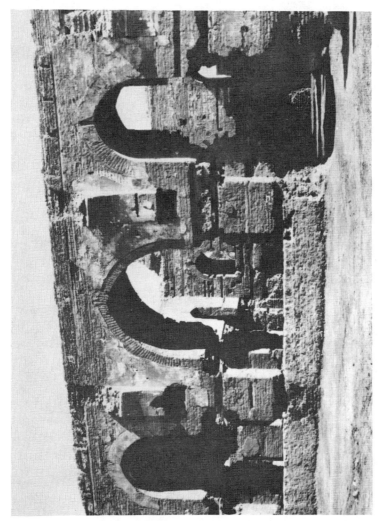

Fig. 2. Triple transept of the mosque of al-Zahir Baybars (1915). Courtesy of the Visual Collections, Fine Arts Library, Harvard University.

Fig. 3. Detail of the northern wall of the mosque of al-Zahir Baybars (1915).
Courtesy of the Visual Collections, Fine Arts Library, Harvard University.

Safety Evaluation and Restoration Techniques of Islamic Monuments

Giorgio Croci

The main problem in the study of monuments is that they are often very complex structures that have usually suffered substantial damage and have deteriorated badly over time.[*] All of this must be investigated thoroughly before intervention can commence. Therefore, the first step must be to examine what has caused cracks and failures in the past and thus find out how the deterioration has developed. The second step, the assessment of the present state, uses this knowledge as a basis for evaluating the safety levels of the building. Observation of the weak zones also provides useful information for the design of the restoration work. Finally, it is necessary to evaluate the safety levels attained after intervention so that they will be neither weaker nor stronger than necessary, as every intervention not only represents a cost but also an alteration to the original concept and therefore must be minimized. Unfortunately, today's scientific knowledge does not allow us to work out these problems completely; we are thus obliged to take into account both subjective and objective aspects, as the rationality of science must be enlarged and tempered by intuition and interpretation of different phenomena.

The Processes of Observation, Analysis, and Historical Research in Intervention

An understanding of a structure's present structural condition can be developed through (1) observation of the existing situation, (2) mathematical analysis, and (3) a historical survey.

Observation of the existing situation is a process which we may call the "empirical-qualitative method," and is in a survey of the monument as it stands today, through the observation of the quality of the materials, the crack and failure patterns, the foundation system, the ground morphology, and so on. This information can be supplemented by chemical and mechanical tests

---

*This paper was prepared with the cooperation of Dott. Ing. Mario Briritognolo and the assistance of Lesley Goldfinger B., Eng.

and by data recorded on a monitoring system in order to highlight the evolution of various phenomena.

The information gained in this process is linked to a subjective interpretation of the present reality and is based on a comparison between what is now observed and what we have observed in the past in other constructions. From a philosophical point of view, this approach can be included in the "inductive process category" upon which the observation of a great number of structures, failures, and phenomena can lead to generalizations and thus, by means of synthesis, to a progressive enlargement whose base is in experience. It was following this process that ancient builders were able to realize great works in the past.

Mathematical analysis is a process which we will call the "theoretical quantitative method." It is based on an evaluation of the strain and stress levels corresponding to different kinds of action (dead and live loads, temperature, soil settlement, earthquakes, etc.). In order to better understand the validity of these criteria, which from a philosophical point of view can be included in the "deductive process category," it is necessary to focus on the structural problems. In so doing we carefully represent the real situation and are able to introduce the simplifications necessary to use the theories we have at our disposal.

The problem represents a central point in the philosophy and in every cognitive process in metaphysics as well as in epistemology: the possibility of connecting the subject with the object, the activity proceeding from the mind of man with reality. From the conceptual point of view, an important step has been realized by the doctrine of "schematism" elaborated by Emanuel Kant in his *Critique of Pure Reason*. In his theory, he attempts to overcome this apparent incommunicability by introducing an intermediate abstract element, the "scheme," which is accessible to the subject and representative of the object. In epistemology, schematism is posed as a problem of scientific models, which are not only logical and mathematical constructions but also representations or imaginary pictures (i.e., schemes) of extremely complex structures. The scheme is located between theory and reality and is thus the only element capable of giving conceptual order and logical rigor to scientific knowledge.

Often in the study of monuments, the identification of a rigorous scheme is unfortunately very difficult. If it is too close to reality (e.g., taking into account interaction with the soil, the possibility of slide between masonry blocks under seismic action and the consequent dissipation of energy, the progressive influence over the centuries of the permanent deformations and deteriorations of the materials, etc.), it is impossible to analyze with reliable theories. On the other hand, the schemes that can be analyzed by current histories can seldom represent all aspects of reality and the phenomena that have occurred. Therefore, a compromise is necessary. According to the philosopher Gaston Bachelard in *Le Rationalisme Applique*, "a knowledge of the non-rigorous must be restored so that a full comprehension of the rigorous may be possible."

Although the elastic finite element models (figs. 1, 2, 3) only provide an approximate explanation of the reality and thus of the failures that have occurred over the centuries, they may be used as an instrument to contribute to the interpretation of reality itself and provide useful information about the zones at risk. Comparison with historical information and the actual situation allows us to provide reliable evaluations.

Last but not least is the historical survey. This process is the basis of real knowledge of a monument. History provides an experimental laboratory on a real scale that we have yet to discover and decode by research, review, and interpretation of historical documents, writings, drawings, and photographs. The main difficulty is that history was not written for structural engineering purposes and thus the objectivity of the facts must be partially rebuilt through the subjective analysis of the researcher. One aspect of the historical survey is to point out occurrences and events that have influenced the structural behavior producing cracks and collapses. The aim of the historical analysis has been the connection between the physical phenomena, especially seismic action, and the damage and failures visible in the monument.

Investigations and Monitoring

Investigations provide a very useful support for the deeper knowledge of the soil conditions, building materials, connection details, and so forth. Thus, they contribute to more reliable data and hence more reliable results related to the criteria mentioned above.

An accurate survey of the geometric characteristics, the crack patterns, and other failure phenomena will be indispensable, to begin with. After this, soil test reports are crucial. If the information available about the soil beneath the foundations is incomplete or totally missing, it is impossible to know the characteristics of the soil and whether there are some phenomena in evolution at the moment. The geometric investigation and geo-technical surveys will first of all allow us to determine the stratigraphic characteristics of the different layers of soil as well as their physical and mechanical properties and the level of the water table.

Some tests for the chemical and physical classification of the materials (stone or brick and fill) will be useful, combined with some tests for the resistance and homogeneity of the masonry. Other investigations regarding the timber structures and the restoration of the decoration and architectural elements will have a general influence, especially in monuments where the architectural features are very important or seriously damaged. Some of the more interesting tests used are endoscopy, sonic testing, penetration testing, and flat jack testing.

Monitoring systems can be useful in the case of evolutionary phenomena. A case of particular interest is that of soil settlements where a radical solution generally involves the underpinning of the building using micropiles; a solution that is, however, very expensive. In order to limit or avoid this kind of intervention, it is necessary to find out if the phenomena of deformation are evolutionary or stabilized, and if evolutionary, their rate of growth and general trend. A monitoring system can control the evolution of cracks, out of plumb, soil deformations, water table variations, etc.

In this way it would be possible to design the minimum reinforcement necessary for the foundation structures and to control the structural behavior before and during the work and only in the case where the evolution is unfavorable, to improve the reinforcement. This philosophy, which may appear unusual in structural engineering, is similar to that applied in the field of medicine, where the physician generally begins with mild drugs to cure an illness and, depending on the patient's response, increases the dosage or decides on surgical intervention.

The monitoring technique is applicable to a vast field of structures with notable benefits for the designers, who may use the objective data on the progression of phenomena as the basis for determining type and degree of urgency of intervention. There are three main fields of application in structural engineering. The first is the preliminary study to define the design of the strengthening work. This consists of checking the evolution of cracks, which of those are connected to cyclical phenomena, such as the rise of ground water or the variation in temperature and therefore the thermal deformations or the progressive phenomena, settlement of the foundations, weakening of the mechanical characteristics of the materials, ground movements, etc.

The second is checking a building, a work of art, or an area during the execution of partial interventions on it or on adjacent zones (variation of loads, underpinnings, deep excavations, gallery passages, etc.). In these cases, the presence of a network of instruments allows the determination of some of the preventive interventions, the execution of temporary structures, or even the temporary abandonment of the site. At the same time the necessary margins of safety are maintained. Whenever signals from the instruments indicate an unfavorable situation, the network acts as a warning bell allowing decisions to be made at an early stage before damage occurs to either people or things.

The third application of structural engineering is to verify at the end of the intervention that it has been as effective as foreseen in the design of the strengthening work or that the phenomena of degradation that took place before the intervention has been halted.

The static type of monitoring, characterized by a base frequency of acquisition (from seconds to days) has the function of determining the evolution, over time, of the size of physical phenomena such as:
— deformation of the structural elements: supporting walls, columns, arches, arch ties or reinforcements, etc.
— Rigid movements: variations in the size of cracks, rotations, differential or absolute settlements.

— Stresses: increase of the earth pressures on walls, variations in the value of tension in ties or reinforcement bars, variations in groundwater pressure, etc.

Dynamic monitoring is, instead, characterized by a high frequency of acquisition (including milliseconds) and can be subdivided into passive and active monitoring. An example of passive (or seismic) monitoring is a network of sensors that are on standby and come into operation when a seismic action occurs or when triggered by a high wind velocity (in the case of belltowers or slender structures), vibrations (traffic), intense acceleration of soil (seismic). Active monitoring records the size of dynamic actions (natural frequency, modes of vibration, damping, etc.) as a function of an artificially created agitation (oleodynamic or vibrodynamic agitation, small explosive loads).

Techniques Used in Interventions

Monuments are often affected by settling of building foundations related to the variation of the water table. Any solution must therefore involve careful analysis and comprehension of this problem and examination of the possibility of further variations related to hydraulic and sewage conditions in the subsoil. Where the soil settlements are evolutionary, we may proceed following four different techniques (fig. 4)

The first is to act on the soil in order to improve its mechanical characteristics. Jet grouting is an example of this type of intervention. This technique consists of the injection of a mixture of water and cement into the soil at a very high velocity. The treatment results in a consolidation of the soil, creating "stone columns." The jet grouting allows for the creation of a diffused stiffening of the foundation soil, by the placing of overlapping columns near or beneath the existing foundations.

The second technique is to transmit the loads to the deeper layers of soil; the most common example of this is underpinning using micropiles. The micropiles can be directly drilled through the walls or close to them. Reinforcement of the masonry by injection is also required. The technique using micropiles enables the utilization of firmer soil strata for bearing. The micropiles also permit an improvement of the weaker soil strata thanks to the injection procedure. By using appropriate steel tubes with special valves as reinforcement to the micropiles, and by placing the tubes in situ after drilling the hole, creating an outer sheath with the primary injection, it is possible to create bulbs with a secondary injection of cement at medium to high pressure.

The third technique consists of acting on the structure, giving it more strength and stiffness by means of the construction of a concrete slab at the ground level; at different levels the timber floor may be connected to the wall by tie bars.

The fourth technique is very useful when the building is large in plan. It consists of creating joints by cutting the walls and floors in the zones where the cracks are more concentrated. This technique is often used in conjunction with the third one and has the advantage of reducing stress in the structure due to soil deformation and improving the overall strength. Interventions of this kind have been realized successfully in many cases, such as in the Ducal Palace of Genoa (fig. 5).

A solution to the problem of rising damp cannot be realized in a short period. As mentioned above, it is related to the resolution of the general hydraulic problem. However, it is now possible to solve the problem of rising humidity by creating a waterproof layer under the paving and by making horizontal cuts at the base of the walls with a special device and inserting a thin layer of insulating material (fig. 6). This intervention is expensive and should be decided on from a general cost-benefit point of view, taking into account that the solution of this problem will allow the definitive prevention of deterioration of the monument (stone, marble, plaster, woods, decorations, and colors).

As ceilings are often covered with decorated timber elements, a partial and provisional removal of these coverings is necessary in order to control their quality and state of conservation. After the inspection and laboratory tests, it will be decided if some elements will be left in their present state, repaired, or rebuilt (partially or totally) following the original typology and materials.

It is necessary, however, in order to better resist the seismic action and the small soil movements, to ensure the connection between the floors and the walls, and at the same time to improve the stiffness in their own plane; this can be achieved by placing a second order of timber floorboards across the original one (fig. 7). At the same time, between the two orders of timber floor-boards, and over the upper one, some steel strips should be placed and anchored to the walls. The anchorage can be made by inserting steel bars in drilled holes of three centimeters in diameter and injected with appropriate mortar.

In some cases there is a heavy layer of material on the roof of a monument due to previous attempts to insulate and seal leaks. As this does not fulfill its purpose and at the same time adds to the dead load, it is often advisable to remove this heavy material and to substitute for it a layer of high density polystirol, which is both lighter and provides very good thermal insulation, and then set in place a waterproof material.

Paving is often cracked due to thermal movements and may have to be replaced—possibly using the same material but being careful to provide a larger spacing between them, filled by mortar in order to avoid the phenomenon described above.

Often walls are not well connected to each other, especially in the corners, where severe cracks may have developed. This lack of structural continuity reduces the global resistance to earthquakes, so that it is necessary to recreate the continuity. Some different solutions can be proposed and the choice can be decided depending of the situation (fig. 8).

— Removal of decayed timber tie-beams and replacement with connected new beams of good-quality wood. The connection will be with thin steel strips protected with zinc to avoid corrosion.

— Removal of some stone blocks and replacing of others in such a way as to ensure connection with the perpendicular wall.

— When there are no wood ties, it is possible to use new technology that involves drilling the masonry (using a nonvibrating machine) and inserting corrosion-proof steel bars or synthetic fiber ropes and injecting an appropriate mortar.

Often the continuity of the walls has been lost due to the presence of serious vertical cracks. When continuity and tensile strength are required, it is necessary to replace the ancient chains or ties that may have held the building together. When this is impossible or insufficient, according to the results of the mathematical models, it may be necessary to insert prestressed cables within the thickness of the floors, roof, and along the nearby walls to prevent any further deformation (fig. 7). This solution was successfully applied in several monuments in Italy. The anchorage of the walls is achieved, as in the case of block-work, by the removal of a part, or the whole, of a block and, in the case of brick-work, by the creation of a cut. After the tensioning of the cables, the block or masonry is replaced and replastered.

Important permanent deformation observed in walls, arches, and columns may be totally or partially recovered using jacks and interposing sandboxes or other soft material after the underlaying causes have been remedied (figs. 9, 10).

Usually in stone block-work monuments, cracks in the materials are not present, but strong forces may generate displacement of blocks resulting in the opening of joints (fig. 11). In these cases, the traditional mortar is much too weak and the joints will have to be filled with an appropriate resin mortar. When base materials are of poor quality, or of masonry composed of two external layers with internal filling, it is necessary to inject not only the cracks but also the fill material, in order to improve the strength and homogeneity of the masonry. In these cases, the injection can be made using cement mortar. If ancient plaster or stuccos are present, the usual cement must be avoided because it may produce efflorescence on the surface. Special mortars for these situations are available.

In the zones where there are concentrations of stress, improvements in the strength of the masonry must be integrated with the insertion of transverse steel bars, as in the case of foundations, to resist concentrated loads transmitted by micropiles.

Often masonry walls or domes have plaster in very poor condition on the external surface. In these cases, it is necessary to remove the decayed walls of plaster, check the deterioration of materials, repair or replace the deteriorated or missing elements, and rebuild the plaster using materials similar to the original.

When the stonework has seriously deteriorated, substitution of similar material is required. In some cases, however, in which the deterioration is very serious, it will be sufficient to remove a superficial part and replace it with a new layer of stone connected by appropriate mortar.

On domes, the restoration of external plaster will often be sufficient. In the case of the presence of cracks, when the mathematical model shows that the safety levels are inadequate, stainless steel cables will be placed along the parallels, under the plaster work, in order to recreate the required original circumferential continuity (figs. 12, 13).

On minarets a simple and reversible intervention may consist of placing vertical steel cables or bars when there is great leaning or when the mathematical model indicates structural weakness of the element. For the placing of these cables, small drill holes on the border of the steps will be sufficient. The cable will be lightly prestressed and covered, ensuring durability.

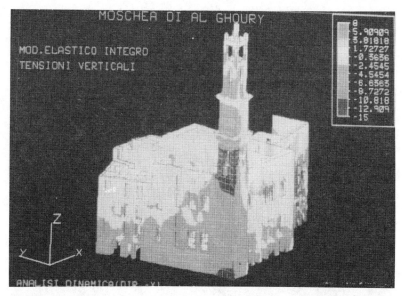

Fig. 1. *Mathematical model of the mosque of al-Ghuri, showing vertical stress levels with seismic action in the x-direction.*

Fig. 2. *Mathematical model with cracks of the mosque of al-Ghuri, showing vertical stress with seismic action in the x-direction.*

Fig. 3. Mathematical model of al-Ghuri mosque with interventions showing vertical stresses with seismic action in the x-direction.

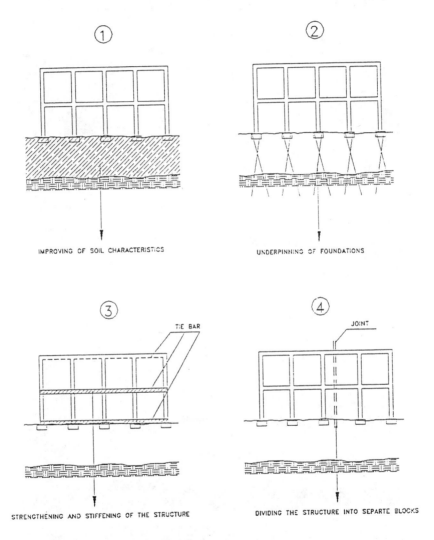

Fig. 4. Interventions to the foundations.

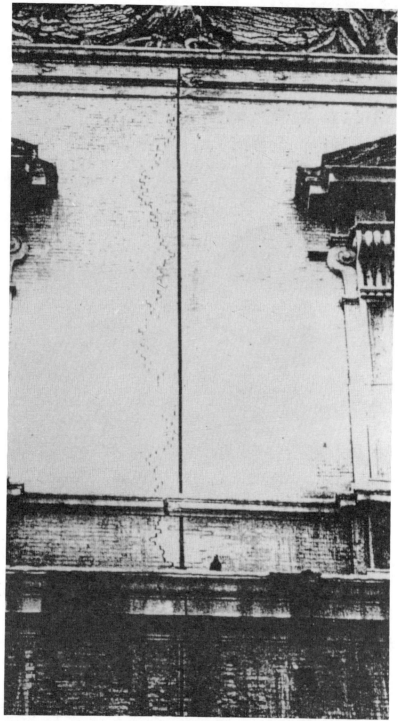

Fig. 5. Cut in the wall of the Ducal Palace of Genoa.

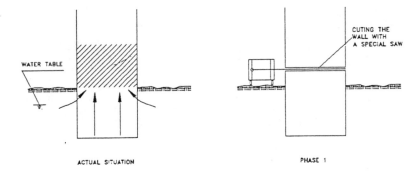

WATER TABLE

CUTING THE
WALL WITH
A SPECIAL SAW

ACTUAL SITUATION

PHASE 1

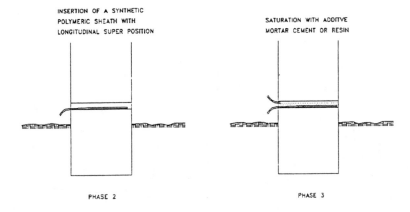

INSERTION OF A SYNTHETIC
POLYMERIC SHEATH WITH
LONGITUDINAL SUPER POSITION

SATURATION WITH ADDITVE
MORTAR CEMENT OR RESIN

PHASE 2

PHASE 3

Fig. 6. Interventions to avoid rising of humidity.

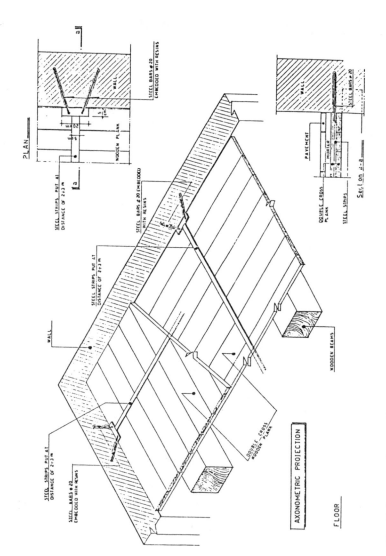

Fig. 7. Interventions to floor structure.

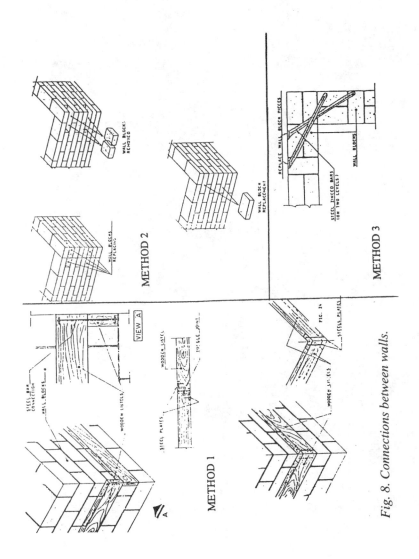

Fig. 8. Connections between walls.

Fig. 9. Leaning column.

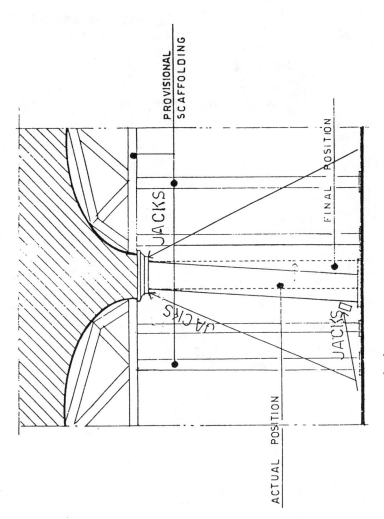

Fig. 10. Repositioning of column.

Fig. 11. Separation of blocks.

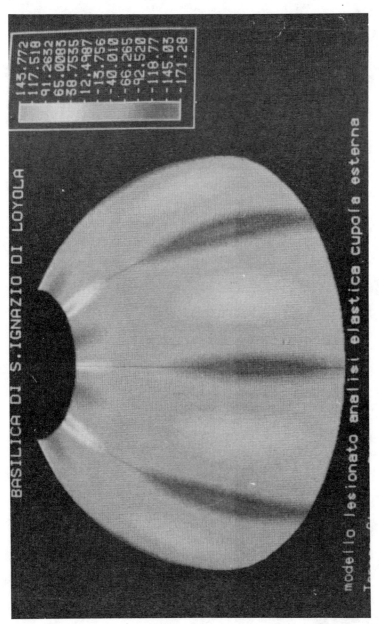

Fig. 12. Mathematical model of the dome of St. Ignatius of Loyola, Spain.

Fig. 13. Placing cables on the dome of St. Ignatius of Loyola, Spain.

A Structural Assessment of Old Domed Masonry Buildings in Seismic Zones

Erhan Karaesmen
Engin Karaesmen

The 12 October 1992 Cairo earthquake created considerable alarm over the condition of Egypt's Islamic architectural heritage. It is important to mention that the only, or at least the main concern, of people who deal with aspects of restoration and conservation of Islamic monuments in Egypt is not specifically old religious buildings in the narrow sense. Islam is a cultural synthesis based on the customs of Arab tribal leadership, Meccan trading oligarchy, Sassanian monarchy, and a legacy of administration from the Byzantines. Later influences on the political concepts evolved out of Mongolian and Turkish traditions. The early Islamic tribes did not intend to encourage religious art. The skilled craftsmen and artists of the conquered lands provided the resources needed to build the earliest religious and secular Islamic buildings. The effect of different cultures (Byzantine, Coptic, Sassanian, Central Asian, Ottoman, etc.) bringing successive waves of influence on the architectural history of Islamic Egypt make the monuments of Egypt and its capital a major cultural site. Their conservation and protection deserve international attention and responsibility.

The first action that should be taken in the conservation process is compiling a list and restoration schedule of the monuments or areas. This phase will to a large degree be dominated by the political, financial, cultural, and educational philosophies of the society concerned. But whatever the decisions on the list, there are some common factors in conservation. In this context, we aim to review (1) the structural engineer's approach to the most frequently used structural material—masonry; (2) the most impressive and representative structural masonry form—the dome; and (3) still the most unavoidable disaster that befalls buildings—the earthquake.

An Overview of Domed Masonry Buildings
The most popular type of building construction all over the world, regardless of historical developments in the architectural arts, is masonry. The great Egyptian

pyramids, Roman, Gothic, Islamic secular and religious buildings, and many others are made of stone, brick, or stone-brick mixed masonry with special mortars. The compressive strength of most stones is quite variable but still far greater than that of masonry in tension, so the structural failure of masonry buildings is not governed by the compression state of stress.

Recent research is attempting to establish a theory for the structural behavior of masonry structures in connection with the existing buildings and their architectural heritage (Baratta and Mengi, et al.). In some of the studies, masonry is modeled as a nontension material or a material with low tensile strength under which brittle rupture is observed. In ancient masonry structures, it has been observed that the order of magnitude of tensile strength of mortars used as grout is less than the masonry itself. Therefore, it is necessary to pay particular attention to mortar. The absence or presence of tension in the mortar and its weakness will greatly affect the structural safety of the masonry structures. Analysis of the microstructure of mortars from Egyptian pyramids, which has been stable over some five thousand years, gives us some idea of the present damage levels and the state of mortar used in them. The mortar of the Cheops pyramid was found to be quick-setting plaster with gypsum microcrystals resulting in long-term stability for the pyramids. In others, a slow-setting mortar has been identified and this is found to be the cause of short-term stability for the pyramid (Regourd, et al.). Recent studies on mortar properties of the Karnak temple resulted in similar findings (Martinet, et al. and Regourd, et al.).

For the Islamic masonry monuments of Egypt, the traditional building materials used are stone for foundations and lower walls, brick for higher and interior walls, and marble for columns. The combined action of masonry blocks and mortar is very important in predicting the strength and deformation characteristics of the constructions. The constituents of the grout, together with the investigations made on the structural elements to locate tensile zones, make it possible to prevent and consolidate distress caused by tension. The masonry-bearing walls may analytically yield small average stresses under earthquake load, but low tensile strength may cause cracks to spread in the wall. Poor and/or deteriorated mortar under sustained shaking action may become a powderlike, ineffective adhesive material with time. The damage should be continuously controlled, bearing in mind that the masonry structures may become highly brittle when cracks are no longer local or small.

Domed roofs, which affect people with their pure, smooth, and solemn geometry, are more than a visual attraction when their structural bearing capacity is considered. For properly designed masonry domes, it may be possible to have no tensile stresses in the direction perpendicular to the meridians of the dome, resulting in an optimum design in the structural sense. As is well known, whether the supports have reactions tangent to the meridian or are arranged in such a way as to impose vertical reactions on the dome where the horizontal components of the meridianal force are taken by a supporting ring, for sufficiently thin domes, the bending effects are of local character. This property of the domes made it possible for master builders of the past to cover large spaces with the use of masonry.

The Pantheon of Rome represented revolutionary progress both in form and material used. The Pantheon is made of an earthen material called *pozzolana*, which was a sort of antique concrete. The Pantheon has a half-spherical dome 43.3 meters in diameter resting over the circular *pozzolana* wall. It has a series of decorative covers on its interior surface. The exterior view of the dome is more conical than spherical due to the increase of thickness of the dome toward its lower edges (fig. 1).

The Hagia Sophia of Istanbul has a different structural form where the huge inner space is covered by the main dome and supported by a series of arches braced by two symmetrical shallower half-cupolas. The partial collapses that occurred even at the time the building was being erected increased during any seismic activity. The external bracings that were introduced did not contribute much to the structural safety of the system. Studies on damage assessment have intensified recently and relevant findings are anticipated.

During the Middle Ages, vaulted forms were extensively used in public and religious halls. Romanesque and Gothic styles of the Western world and Seljuk and Sassanid realizations in the Middle East all adopted enlarged vaults with or without braced ribs and crossing arches. The domes of those periods were rather small and thus the structural stability of tall walls and columns were of more concern and were maintained by the flying buttress systems (Heyman and Mark).

In Egypt, Fatimids, Abbasids and the early Mamluks erected mosques and shrines with iwans, arcades, and aisles in arched form with small cupolas. The domes of the period were of spherical or hexagonal form and were generally constructed of mortared brick. The Coptic churches of medieval times in Egypt also reflect characteristics of Middle Eastern architecture such as brick vaults and flat timber surfaces.

Last but not least in relation to the structural system is the double-skinning technique introduced in the domes. From the Pantheon of Rome to Brunelleschi's dome in the Florence cathedral, many ingenious progressive realizations took place, which maintained the safety of many structures with which we are concerned, except for the misfortune that befell the Hagia Sophia and the collapse of Beauvais. The survival of many of the nonsecular buildings in Egypt is also a good demonstration of the structural techniques of the medieval period.

The most challenging examples of Islamic architecture with domed masonry were realized by the Ottomans. They were able to merge the Byzantine and Seljuk experiences, so as to construct domes or series of domes transmitting the thrust of seismic activity laterally to the massive exterior walls or piers in a very effective way. The great master builder Sinan (A.D. 1492–1588), originally a military engineer, worked for almost half a century as the chief architect of the empire and gave his name to many of the secular and nonsecular buildings and constructions of the period. Sinan seems to have taken advantage of all possible combinations of the domed and arched systems in a very elegant and robust way (fig. 2). Four major edifices that have been considered indicative works in the evolutionary path of Sinan's domical art, are, in chronological order: (1) the Sehzade (Prince) Mehmet mosque (1548), erected at the end of the first phase of a promising career; (2) the Sulaymaniya mosque (1557), considered to be the summit of his passage to the master period; (3) Mihrimah Sultan mosque (1565), considered an extraordinary work from both a structural and architectural point of view; and (4) Selimiye mosque (1575), a true masterpiece, with the largest masonry dome ever constructed.

The Mihrimah Sultan mosque seems to have the most daring structural skeleton as there are no partial cupolas bracing the main dome externally. The transmission and resistance mechanisms for both seismic and gravity activity are ensured by elegant thin arches and pendantives below the main dome in mortared brick masonry having a diameter of 21 meters and at a height of 38 meters above ground. Extensive assessments were done on this edifice. Various comparative finite element models were developed for computer-based analysis. Figure 3 is offered here as an example of contemporary approaches in the idealization of domed masonry structures. It represents one of the detailed models of the Mihrimah Sultan mosque (Karaesmen, et al. and Karaesmen).

Imitating the Ottomans, many architects in Egypt built mosques and minarets of the Ottoman type with forecourts and sanctuaries consisting of half-domes attached to domed cubes surrounded by arches and pendantives. Therefore, findings of the studies on arched and domed masonry skeletons are considered quite relevant to Egyptian Islamic monuments as well.

The problems associated with the restoration and conservation of monuments of a certain period are alike everywhere. The medieval Islamic monuments in Cairo present many structural and architectural features that are familiar to structural or conservation engineers of any origin. The structural safety and integrity of a monument needs to be analyzed and decided by methods based on physical and universal laws. Computational techniques enable us to get overall safety assessments of masonry buildings of any geometry under elastic or inelastic assumptions. Many studies (e.g., Ambrassey and Stiros) show that the orderly or disorderly distribution of masonry pieces do not always indicate the action of earthquakes on the ancient constructions as is the case in many of the monuments in Cairo. Furthermore, it is expected that the soil conditions of Egypt in general are such that the high frequency of ground motion may be filtered by the soil, so only tall buildings of low frequency (e.g., minarets) seem to be vulnerable, and thus require special attention before future earthquakes or any dynamic effect.

Indeed, sophisticated computation techniques to masonry-bearing systems considered elastic or inelastic contribute to the overall assessment. But sometimes more precise information is needed for details of preservation/

protection operations. A more systematic approach, then, is needed to evaluate the behavioral features of old masonry structures with domes. The following steps should be taken in the analysis and restoration of masonry structures: (1) examination of geo-technical features, soil, and foundation elements; (2) determination of detailed geometrical features of the buildings, including foundation components; (3) establishing a monitoring system with systematic permanent measurement of deformations; (4) study of material science, particularly intensified on mortared masonry behavior; (5) evaluation of a detailed structural model and full structural analysis of the bearing system with system identification work if necessary, including all parameters of dynamic response; (6) experimental studies, if considered necessary, on a laboratory model of structures; (7) maintenance of close contact all through the studies with architectural historians and art philosophers to ensure usefulness of findings; (8) interpretation of engineering results with the objective of contributing to preservation practices.

Bibliography

Ambraseys, N. N. "The Assessment of Historical Earthquake in Central Greece." *Proceedings of the Meeting on Earthquakes in the Archaeological Record . . . .* Athens, 13–15 June 1991.

Baratta, A. "Statics and Reliability of Masonry Structures," Lecture Notes, CISM. Udine, 1990.

Heyman, J. "The Stone Skeleton." *Journal of Solid Structures* 2 (1966): 249–79.

Karaesmen, E. "A Study of Sinan's Domed Structures." *Proceedings of First STREMA—Structural Repair and Maintenance of Historic Buildings Conference.* Florence, 1989, pp. 201–10.

Karaesmen, E., C. Erkay, N. Boyaci, and A. I. Unay. "Seismic Behavior of Old Masonry Structures." *Proceedings of the Tenth World Conference on Earthquake Engineering.* Madrid, 1992, pp. 4531–36.

Mark, R. *Experiments in Gothic Structure.* London: MIT Press, 1982.

Martinet, G., F. X. Deloye, and J. C. Golvin. "Caracterisation des mortiers pharaoniques du temple d'Amon à Karnak." *Bulletin de liaison des Laboratories des Pont et Chaussees.* Sept.–Oct. 1992.

Mengi, M., H. D. McNiven, and K. Tanrikulu. "Models for Nonlinear Earthquake Analysis of Brick Masonry Buildings." *Report of Earthquake Engineering Research Center.* University of California, Berkeley. Report No. EER C-92/03, 1992.

Regourd, M. and J. Kerisel. "Microstructure of Mortars from Three Egyptian Pyramids." *Cement and Concrete Research* 18 (1988): 81–90.

Stiros, S. C. "Identification of Prehistoric and Historical Earthquakes from their Effects on Ancient Constructions." *Proceedings of the October 1992 International Seminar on Seismic Effects on Historic Buildings.* Turkish Ministry of Public Works and Settlement. Ankara, 1993.

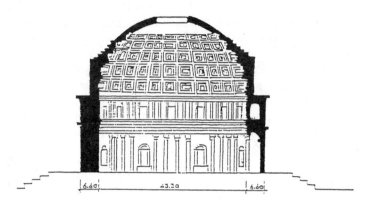

Fig. 1. Descriptive interior section of the Pantheon.

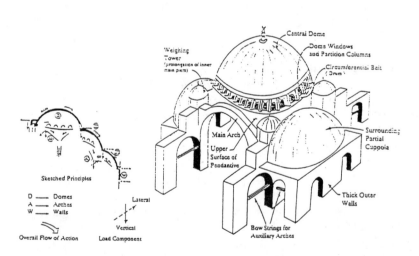

Fig. 2. Typical components and action-flow mechanism in Ottoman domed buildings.

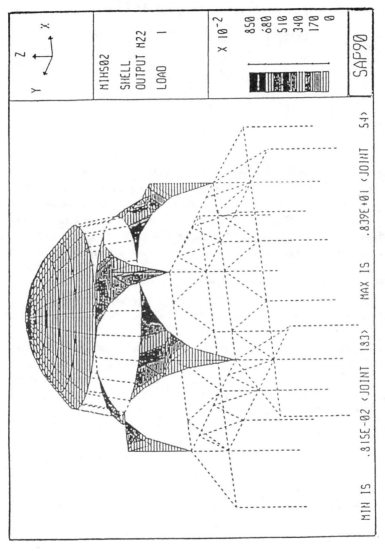

Fig. 3. Full structural model of the Mihrimah mosque, including lower components.

Conservation of the Islamic Monuments of Cairo

Jane Slate Siena

Egyptian Antiquities Organization Chairman Bakr, United States Ambassador and Mrs. Pelletreau, and other distinguished guests, thank you for accepting the invitation to join us this morning to open a conference devoted to the conservation of Cairo's Islamic heritage. We are very pleased to be here on the beautiful campus of the American University in Cairo, and are delighted to have a high attendance from our colleagues from Cairo University, other Egyptian universities, and the Egyptian Antiquities Organization.

The events of 12 October 1992, in Cairo have propelled us into action, and have provided the impetus for all of us to come together at this moment to examine the situation with the hope and, indeed, the goal of developing a realistic plan to conserve the historic zone of Cairo.

The Getty Conservation Institute is a very young organization, founded in 1985 as part of the J. Paul Getty Trust in Los Angeles, California. Our mandate is international, and our mission is to preserve the world's cultural heritage for the enrichment and education of present and future generations. The institute seeks to develop, apply, and make available appropriate solutions to conservation problems through research, training, fieldwork, and the exchange of information. We believe that the world's cultural heritage is essential to the understanding of history and of the forces that create contemporary society. Protecting this heritage is a national and an international responsibility.

The Getty Conservation Institute achieves its mission by developing partnerships with cultural authorities to address their most urgent problems. Today, we have projects in fourteen countries, a staff in Los Angeles from twenty-one nations, a fully equipped conservation laboratory and library, numerous consultants in specialized fields of study, and a visible program of conservation actions in China, Israel, Cyprus, Macedonia, the Czech Republic, Russia, throughout Latin America, and of course Egypt. In each of these countries, we help to make a difference in terms of how people care for their museum and library collections, archaeological sites and objects, and historic architecture.

It has been our great pleasure to work in Egypt since 1986, at the invitation of Dr. Ahmed Kadry and Dr. Gamal Moukhtar. As many of you know, our projects in Egypt include environmental monitoring in the tomb of Nefertari, following its conservation; conservation of the King of Tutankhamun; training of Egyptian conservators in the tomb of Kiki; development of appropriate cases for the Royal Mummy Collection at the Egyptian Museum; and environmental monitoring at the Great Sphinx. Today, we are delighted to enter the realm of the Islamic heritage, by joining the American Research Center in Egypt and the Egyptian Antiquities Organization in hosting this conference.

Our work in conservation is nothing if not urgent. Today the cultural heritage is threatened as never before. Technological innovation and the global population explosions have given rise to uncontrolled development, industrial pollution, increased tourism, rapid obsolescence, and increasingly destructive methods of warfare. As a result, the material evidence of our past is vanishing at an ever-excellerating rate.

Long before Roman times, societies attempted to restore or protect important structures in urban areas. But the survival of the old and historic in today's cities does not reflect any single set of standards or priorities. The long history of urban conservation has yet to produce a consensus on how to balance the goals of conservation with the changing demands of city life. Since 1964, a series of international charters and conventions has been developed to address the long-term preservation of historic cities. Of the more than 350 sites on the World Heritage list today, 73 are historic cities or towns. In July 1991, representatives, including the mayors of 40 of these cities, held their first "International Meeting of World Heritage Cities," in Quebec City; the group will reconvene for its second meeting in September 1993 in Fez. Mayors, architects, and city planners from historic city centers are a new constituency, reflecting the reality of urban growth during our lifetimes and the needs resulting from it.

The reality of contemporary society prompts us to find new solutions to save our cultural heritage. Today, development agencies, banks, private foundations, and local and national governments are more aware of the need to integrate conservation and economic development—seemingly disparate issues in the past. Fortunately, conservation science has evolved sufficiently during this century to provide insights that support new approaches to preservation. Impelled by the explosion of scientific knowledge and an unprecedented worldwide interest in culture, the growth of the conservation field during the latter half of this century has been dramatic. The contribution of science to conservation practice has been not only pivotal, but radical. With it has come a philosophy that recognizes the need for prevention before repair or restoration. Nowhere is this more evident than in the area of disaster preparedness and response, when we witness the collapse or damage of our precious monuments which may owe more to the monuments' fragile condition than to the earthquake itself. Much of our heritage is located in seismic zones, a fact that inspired Sir Bernard Feilden to publish, with the Getty Conservation Institute, his work, *Between Two Earthquakes: Cultural Property in Seismic Zones.* For we do indeed live at all times between disasters of one kind or another. The Getty Conservation Institute has been at the forefront of research on both the effects of the environment and disaster preparedness and response on the cultural heritage. At this conference Dr. Neville Agnew will review the range of work at the Getty Conservation Institute on the topic of disaster preparedness, related to buildings and to museum collections.

Finally, I want to say how fortunate I feel to have the chance to come here and walk through your historic zone, in both daytime and at night. Inspired by the brilliantly nuanced stories of Naguib Mahfouz, I have for some time dreamed of knowing Cairo. Yesterday, I closed my eyes on the now immortalized street called Palace Walk, and tried to imagine myself sitting in the latticed balconies, anticipating and absorbing the small pleasures of life. We passed the great stone monuments where people have prayed for centuries; and the shops and cafes where millions of people have made their fortunes and their pleasures. The historic zone of Cairo blends the secular and the spiritual in a very special way. The zone has retained its sense of community and commerce. From the medieval minaret of the Qalawun mosque, one enjoys a sensational view of the Citadel and the old city wall. This view encompasses the households of what must be millions. The monochromatic hue of sand and sand-colored structures produces a staggering sight—a mirage of a city, an imagined existence for some, and an all-too-real lifestyle for so many others.

We are obliged to tackle the difficult problems of historic city conservation. It is here where the cultural sector can have an impact on the quality of life of our cities and of our citizens.

The Spirit of the Conference

Mark M. Easton

When we were considering the goals for this conference before the earthquake of 12 October 1992, our aims were modest indeed. We conceived of the conference as a small working group of experts, who would discuss the technical problems associated with the conservation of Islamic monuments, identify several monuments for restoration, publish a report, and seek someone to undertake restoration. Simplicity itself—a wonderful exercise in American pragmatism. If it's broke, fix it.

Fortunately, the American Research Center in Egypt (ARCE) embraces more than thirty-six major American institutions, whose members are experts and specialists in many disciplines. Additionally I have somehow attracted good friends, both Egyptian and expatriate. All gently sought to remedy my state of hopeful ignorance. Then the earthquake brought a new urgency to the situation.

On the financial and administrative side, the small stream of USIA money was joined by powerful institutions, both Egyptian and American, and ideas and support from many individuals from a variety of countries, until we had a flash flood of support.

What emerged was the realization that this is not a matter of a quick fix. There is a much greater agenda than we initially thought. *Nonetheless there is a great lesson here.* We must seek to be as inclusive as possible, to tap the talents of many, and to coordinate different attitudes, personalities, and institutions, if we are to make a difference. This may be a more difficult task than the actual restoration itself. It must be done.

I want to state that if there are people absent who should be here, if I have violated protocol of rank or position, or have otherwise offended, this is due to the short time I have been in Egypt and budget constraints.

ARCE may have a role in bringing ideas, institutions, and people together. We want to raise a large tent, and bring under it all those who seek to see the great heritage of Islamic Egypt saved. We do not seek to dominate, but we may have a role to facilitate. Our tent must also include those who came before us, and the great work they have done. Their recommendations remain with us still.

My own view is that this past work must be rapidly reviewed, its recommendations reconsidered, and note taken of what has been implemented and what recommendations should be implemented. There is a considerable body of literature, much of which may not be immediately available, but it is known to this audience, and others. We need to centralize that information, and I urge you to supply it to us. We in turn will establish a permanent archive at the new ARCE facility for use by those engaged in the conservation process. We have already brought together the 1980 UNESCO report, published papers of the 1978 conference, and many of the reports produced by international teams after the 12 October 1992 earthquake. We will reproduce all these materials at cost for anyone who needs them for his or her work.

Now certain truths must be acknowledged. *First*, the monuments of Islamic Egypt and particularly historic Cairo do not belong to ARCE, or other foreign institutions. They are not the property of *all* even if they do represent part of the world's historic heritage. They belong to Egypt. What is done to them or not done are decisions that ultimately must be made by Egyptians. Should Egypt seek assistance and advice, many of us may be able, in the spirit of friendship, to help.

Second, recommendations are of little value if they cannot be implemented, or are not implemented. If we are to see Cairo's historic zone conserved, we must enter into a renewed dialogue with the appropriate Egyptian officials, a dialogue that distinguishes between the *desirable* and the *possible*.

Third it is necessary actually to do the possible. Many of you are already engaged in this process. The earthquake last October makes it urgent that we move ahead. There is little inherently wrong with the recommendations of the 1980 UNESCO report, and of the several that have followed it. There is general agreement that the *Venice Charter* and *Lahore Statement* principles have merit, and that they should be acknowledged and used.

One recommendation of the 1980 UNESCO report is that the water level of historic Cairo be brought under control and lowered. Few object to this. Most recognize that it must be done. What is not always stated is that if it is done hastily or wrong, this act, necessary as it is, could result in serious damage to numerous monuments. This major problem must be worked through. I use this as but one example of the tough decisions that are out there. This is not going to be a quick fix. So do we simply conclude our conference, issue our report, and walk away? Is that enough? We think not.

We are going to have to try to establish a permanent dialogue. We are going to have to focus on recommendations. We are going to have to focus on implementation, and we are going to have to focus on quality control and damage limitation. It has to be done right.

The final session of this conference has been reserved for general discussion of the issues and recommendations. Let no one believe that the dialogue will not be political, economic, social, technical, and archaeological. It will be all of this and more.

Furthermore, we have a flexible and moving definition of what is "right." Even when we think we have it right, we must hang out a sign reading "honest critics welcome," because they may have caught something we missed. The prize for doing our job well is the rescue of an entire medieval town. We should remember that Europe has lost most of its medieval monuments (and the United States never had any). We are simply urging Egypt not to take the same path. As part of the dialogue we need to establish advisory panels.

While there is much to be done, one of the purposes of this conference is to show that *much has been done*, and that *much has been done extremely well*. This is true not only in restoration but in the dialogue process. Success is possible. We need more of it. We need to praise our colleagues for what they have accomplished. We need to put some hope and energy behind a strengthened effort. We need to be intelligent about it, and *very careful*. And speaking of praise, right at the start, you need to know that the two people who "made it happen" in terms of this conference are Jere Bacharach and Barbara Fudge, who have spent months on the preparations.

We welcome you here today. We honor your past contribution, we welcome your help in the future, and hope this forum will be the start of a dynamic new dialogue, and yes, I have to say it, something practical.

For now let me urge you to let the dialogue begin.

Resolutions of the International Conference on the Restoration and Conservation of Islamic Monuments in Egypt

15 June 1993
Cairo, Egypt

Whereas a primary purpose of the International Conference is to foster and support the current Egyptian Antiquities Organization (EAO) initiative, including international cooperation, toward restoration and conservation of Islamic monuments and

Whereas all resolutions were voted on by over seventy participants, it is resolved that:

1. The historic sites and monuments in greatest danger need urgent and immediate intervention. As emergency repairs are implemented, structures should be monitored to assess the effectiveness of the repairs.

2. The Egyptian Antiquities Organization is urged to establish a mechanism for prioritizing those monuments and historic sites that need restoration; and in the selection of projects, priority should be given to buildings that have a mixed and sustainable use, including sustainable maintenance.

3. There should be regular recording of individual structures, including their archaeology, that is, the changes that have been made to the monuments over time. Defects should be monitored and specific details dictating conservation methods for each structure should be recommended.

4. Existing, as well as new scientific and historical data should be consolidated. Knowledge of soil conditions, ground water, stone types, mortar composition, geology, photogrammatry, and seismic threat should be ac-

quired and fed into data-banks that can be shared by concerned institutions and scholars. Preservation of existing documents referring to the monuments, especially waqfiya, should be undertaken. It is urged that updated computer equipment and software programs be maintained by the Center for Documentation for Islamic and Coptic Monuments.

5. In order to safeguard the special nature of the historic urban environment, an integrated approach to conservation should be adopted. This approach may be initiated through the identification of one or two pilot project areas. Special historic areas should be designated in order to provide clear guidelines for the planning and control of development in these areas. In these special historic areas, effective liaison with local communities may result in useful community involvement in the conservation and repair of buildings.

6. The list of monuments and archaeological sites needs to be updated on a continuous basis with particular attention paid to surveying the monuments and archaeological sites outside Cairo. Monuments not on the current EAO list, but identified at the conference and submitted to the EAO, should be given high priority.

7. As the number of protected buildings grows, methods to encourage and regulate the owners and/or occupants should be designed by the EAO to ensure that they take an active part in the care of the historic sites and monuments.

8. A program should be established to make historical knowledge available to the general public by such means as identifying monuments on the EAO list with plaques giving the name of the site and the date when the building was constructed in both Arabic and English.

9. An appreciation of the cultural heritage of Egypt from all periods needs to be included in the Ministry of Education programs. Scholars, particularly those in faculties of arts and archaeology of Egypt's universities, should be involved in creating teaching classroom modules, material specific for the sites, and developing programs addressed to the general public in such media as television.

10. Ideas to stimulate further training initiatives should be explored, and, in particular, the role of craftsmen needs to be encouraged as part of the current repair program.

11. Where appropriate, material for low-technology seismic retrofit such as diaphragm action of roofs, tying perimeter walls, and vertically tying of tops of minarets and parapet walls should be installed.

12. In light of the critical situation resulting from the 12 October 1992 earthquake and Cairo's rising water level, the Egyptian Antiquities Organization may wish to review its operations and procedures to strengthen its personnel and resources in order to meet the unprecedented challenges ahead.

Contributors

Abd El-Zaher A. Abo El-Ela, *Department of Conservation, Faculty of Archaeology, Cairo University*

M. Abou Kefa, *Department of Public Works, Faculty of Engineering, Cairo University*

Mohamed Ahmed Awad, *Egyptian Antiquities Organization, Cairo*

Irene A. Bierman, Department of Art History, *University of California-Berkeley, Los Angeles, California*

Giorgio Croci, *University of Rome, Rome, Italy*

Jaroslaw Dobrowolski, *Polish Center of Archaeology, Cairo*

Mark Easton, *American Research Center in Egypt, Cairo*

Giuseppe Fanfoni, *Centro per la Formazione Professionale in Restauro, Rome, Italy*

Daryl Fowler, *The Conservation Practice, West Sussex, England*

A. A. Abdel Gawad, *Department of Engineering, Faculty of Engineering, Cairo University*

Mohammed Abd El-Hady, *Department of Conservation, Faculty of Archaeology, Cairo University*

Nairy Hampikian, *German Archaeological Institute, Cairo, Egypt*

M. S. Hilal, *Department of Engineering, Faculty of Engineering, Cairo University*

Engin Karaesmen, *Middle East Technical University, Ankara, Turkey*

Erhan Karaesmen, *Middle East Technical University, Ankara, Turkey*

Saleh Lamei, *Centre for Conservation and Preservation of Islamic Architectural Heritage, Cairo*

David Look, *Preservation Assistance Branch, National Parks Service, San Francisco, California*

Medhat al-Minabbawy, *Egyptian Antiquities Organization, Cairo*

Ahmed Ouf, *Department of Architecture, Faculty of Engineering, Cairo University*

Jane Slate Siena, *Getty Conservation Institute, Malibu, California*

Philipp Speiser, *Historical Archaeologist and Restorer, Fribourg, Switzerland*

Index